Living in Tandem

A Memoir About Being More Than An Autism Mom

By Audrey Burt Saha

All photos from family sources.
Slam poem by Manisha Saha.

Cover art: Painting by Keyan Saha.
Cover and book design by Saw-mon and Natalie.
Layout by Laura Kelsey.
Editing by Zoe McKenna, Mali Bain, and Daphne Ffoulkes-Jones.
Copyediting by Kerry Davie.

Published by NextGen Story: Custom Publishing
www.nextgenstory.com

Living in Tandem

Table of Contents

PART II
THE MIDDLE—FEELS LIKE A FIGHT

PART III
AWAKENING TO PEACE AND HARMONY

"I was once afraid of people saying,
'Who does she think she is?'
Now I have the courage to stand and say
'This is who I am.'"

-Oprah Winfrey

Dedication

This book is dedicated to my loves Kunal, Manisha, and Keyan. Thank you for continuing to journey with me.

Preface

A writer's dilemma: Where to start? Do I begin with the moment he receives a diagnosis that shatters our hearts, hopes, and dreams into a million pieces? When we realize that raising our perfect little chunky, cherub-like child would be something totally unscripted? It is important for me to get this right. After all, this is my life being told openly, candidly, and authentically for all to read. I want to bring you along on a journey of unexpected self-discovery initiated by the presence of autism in my life. Those of you who have followed me on social media over the span of fifteen years will be familiar with some of the stories I tell, but will discover new ones too. For those of you who don't know me: welcome. This is my journey of struggling to be seen, heard, and supported as a mom to a boy–actually a young adult–with autism.

Although I have been putting pen to paper and tapping away on the keys of my MacBook for years now, I have still wrestled with writing this book for many reasons. The biggest obstacle was the lack of belief in my abilities to do it. So many times the devil intruded on my thoughts, creeping in to remind me that I was not good enough or smart enough to rise to the challenge. Constant chatter in my head put into question whether or not people cared enough to read my story. What tipped the scales was the endless stream of private messages I received from people reaching out with the kindest words of encouragement when I went from posting on Facebook to writing a blog on my very own website. I finally made the decision once and for all to commit to writing this book. Yet, during the writing process, I continued to get in my own way. It is through the support of my family, close friends, and the connections I have made via social media that I have been able to keep writing and complete this book.

In the spring of 2020, I spent three months sitting outside at the break of every dawn working on the book. I was in the perfect state of flow, excited to wake up every day to new possibilities. Sometimes I would write about autism and other times I would merely write about what was on my mind. There were times my writing sessions revolved around sharing my deepest thoughts and inner truths. While I was writing, I was expanding and developing a growth mindset. I found a freedom different from any kind that I had ever known. I thought I was writing a book about autism, but it evolved into something more. I gave myself the space to write about whatever I was experiencing without censorship. The result is this book that journeys through motherhood, the early days of coming to terms with my son's autism, the birth of a charitable organization, a life spent running to and from things, and the messy parts of awakening to my own life.

I believe COVID-19 saved me. Mere weeks before the pandemic shut everything down, I was on the verge of a total burnout. I was utterly exhausted and unmotivated by the work I was doing at Soutien Autisme Support

(S.Au.S), a charitable organization I founded in 2009. The organization's mission is to help create leisure programs for autistic individuals who did not fit into normal settings. It was my way of making space in the world for my son and others just like him. I wanted my son to experience the same kind of childhood as everyone else–filled with sports, leisure, and camp. Over the years, the amount of time and energy required to build, grow, and maintain the organization with little outside financial support from the government and corporate groups made the pressure on me insurmountable. I was struggling, and no one was throwing me a lifeline. In order for the organization to move in the direction I wanted it to, which was to build sustainable programs for adults on the severe end of the autism spectrum, I needed to build an impossible relationship with the Quebec government.

Introduction

COVID-19 had all of Quebec shut down in March 2020. It was hard to accept, but an emergency meeting with the board of directors clarified that the Autism Awareness Run scheduled for Sunday, April 26, 2020 would be cancelled. I could hardly breathe—it was so painful. But instead of trying to control the situation, I totally surrendered. In letting go, I found space to ask some really hard questions. How much longer could I do this work? Why was I still trying to do it? Would I burn myself out? My ego kept me going, although my heart had nothing left to give. I sat outside under the sun on a cool spring day and asked myself this question: If I only had one year left on this earth—would I have regrets?

The answer was a resounding hell yeah! It would be a heart-wrenching regret of mine if I put the needs of S.Au.S. before being there for my own children. When I started S.Au.S., I was trying to create a life for Keyan outside of home and school. I desperately wanted him to have opportunities that neurotypical children had. A fun-filled childhood. I was determined to create that for him. As the years went on, it seemed more and more difficult to get Keyan to participate. Once he reached adolescence, he no longer wanted to be involved in soccer, dance, or music. He went less and less. Staying home is what made him happy. It felt as though I was doing all this work for nothing. My motivation disappeared. I worked on a volunteer basis, which meant my motivation had to be something other than financial remuneration. Throughout the twelve years with S.Au.S, I never drew a salary. Keyan and Manisha have always been my biggest motivators—my raison d'être. They make me want to be the best human being I can possibly be. When Keyan lost interest in S.Au.S. programs, I did too. But I had a dark cloud hanging over me—what would Keyan's future look like if I decided to walk away from it all?

The organization I had started, which once filled me with a tremendous passion and desire to help others, now felt like the most suffocating place for me to be. I used to refer to S.Au.S. as my third child. That is how committed I was to the work and the cause. It was hard to admit, but it was time to let go. The work was chipping away at me. The only obstacle was the fear of letting everyone down. I was walking away before delivering what I had promised—a center to house day programs for adults. I had spent the better part of five years working towards that goal and encouraging people to rally around it. I pushed my own needs aside in order to push the agenda forward. Sadly, I could no longer keep up the pace and it felt like it was all crashing down. I was on the verge of a complete breakdown and I had to protect my mental, physical, and emotional well-being. My ego told me that my value was tied up in the work I was doing for the autism community, but my soul knew better. As for my family, who would take care of them if something happened to me? I knew that if I didn't take care of myself first, I couldn't care for my children either—and no one else could step into that role. Ironically, I created the organization for my family and would leave for them too.

While homeschooling Keyan during the worldwide shutdown, I had several light bulb moments. Simply put, with no more obligations—no work, no fundraising, no activities—there was no life outside of the home. Every day I woke up with the goal of getting through it: taking care of Keyan. I have to be honest, this terrified me. The amount of energy it takes to care for Keyan on a day-to-day basis is enormous. It is utterly exhausting, to be totally frank. To meet a person's needs minute by minute takes a tremendous amount of patience, stamina, and resilience. A lot of the time it's not fun. Ironically, it was during this time that I learned to become even more patient with him. It was up to me to find ways that could help both of us learn to live in harmony and get the most out of every day. I created a small routine that helped ground us both. I admit I do like structure with small variances. Keyan is very much the same. Over the course of our time together, removing the veil of autism revealed his true character as that of an introvert, someone who likes a chosen few, with a preference towards one-on-one activities. As we adjusted to this new life at home, Keyan became calmer and happier overall. It became evident that he loves his family and feels best in his home environment.

This book is a labour of love and an extension of my work at S.Au.S. (raising awareness for the autism community). It shows my undying devotion to my family, and my strong desire to grow as a woman. My wish is for you to get inside these stories and to viscerally feel the beauty, frustration, joy, pain, patience, resilience, sacrifice, and love within my struggles.

Living in Tandem was originally intended to be a book solely about Keyan and his autism, but as I wrote, the stories expanded. That is why I decided to write the book in three parts:

Part I–Figuring Out How to Be a Special Needs Mom
This part is about our autism journey, beginning with the diagnosis, moving towards figuring out how to parent Keyan. It is also about my transitioning from mom (private life) to autism activist (public life).

Part II–The Middle—Feels Like a Fight
In this part I share stories about the highs and lows we experience in our day-to-day lives, sprinkled with incredible accomplishments and wins.

Part III–Awakening to Peace and Harmony
This section is all about rethinking and reimagining our future, now guided by the desire to live in peace and harmony. I have a new vision for Keyan's future and it all has to do with living in harmony with one another.

Over the years I have shared our autistic life on social media in an attempt to feel less alone. At this point in my life and my advocacy work, it was important for me to share my story in a more permanent way—hence the writing of this book. Putting *Living in Tandem* out into the world is an ode to my beautiful children and my loving husband, Kunal, and an attempt to honour the hard work I put into making a difference.

When I close my eyes and picture someone leafing through the pages of this book with my words strung together, it truly is a dream come true.

PART I

Figuring Out How to Be a Special Needs Mom

With Just a Call

It all started when my baby boy was suffering from chronic ear infections. Tired of pumping him up with prescription drugs, after the fifth round of antibiotics I insisted that the pediatrician refer Keyan to an ear, nose, and throat specialist (ENT). Without hesitation, the ENT scheduled Keyan to have tubes inserted into his ears. A few weeks after this procedure, the specialist ordered an audiology exam, simply to ensure that everything was okay and that Keyan's issues were solved. Little did we know that this exam would usher in a whole new beginning.

During the audiology exam, Keyan was extremely uncooperative so they decided to schedule an appointment at the Montreal Children's Hospital the following week. Here again, Keyan was uncooperative. Not to worry, they had another type of technology to determine whether or not he could hear us. The test concluded that he could. They proceeded to ask me a list of questions. At the time, I was simply relieved that my son was not deaf. I didn't overthink things. Two days after our visit to the audiology clinic at the children's hospital, the phone rang. It was the pediatrician. Seconds into this conversation, he revealed that the audiologist had picked up on several red flags and suspected that Keyan might have autism. That is how the news was delivered to me: a phone call that shattered my perfect little life.

I would spend the next several weeks with my head in a fog. All I knew was that I needed to figure out how to get him to see a doctor who could tell me officially if Keyan was autistic or not. After all, the pediatrician said the audiologist suspected autism, but it wasn't her field of expertise. Only a neuro-psychologist had the tools to make a proper diagnosis.

There is no cure for autism. A report of the National Autism Spectrum Disorder Surveillance System (Canadian Government Data Blog, 2018, https://health-infobase. canada.ca/datalab/autism-blog.html) says:

It is a complex life-long condition that impacts not only the person with ASD, but their families, caregivers, and communities. Each person with an Autism Spectrum Disorder (ASD) is unique and will have different symptoms, deficits, and abilities. Because of the range of characteristics, this condition is called a "spectrum" disorder, where one's abilities and deficits can fall anywhere along a spectrum, and thereby, support needs may range from none to very substantial.

Grieving

There was an all-consuming, frantic sense of urgency to get Keyan diagnosed. It kept me awake most nights. If Keyan was to get the services he needed from the public health system, he needed to obtain an "official" autism diagnosis. These services include: speech therapy (providing tools for non-speaking communication), occupational therapy (to help with fine and gross motor skills, along with sensory issues), and ABA therapy (applied behavioural analysis therapy—a proven therapy to help individuals with autism learn to decode the world).

Every doctor's office I called didn't seem to understand the urgency. I needed to explain how "early intervention is key." I hoped the receptionist on the phone would sense my desperation and feel sorry for me, giving me the next available appointment. The response was always that they would put Keyan's name on their waiting list. When I asked how long it would take for his name to be called up, the answer was, "About a year." That answer always sent me into a state of panic. The only way I could make my son better or as close to normal as possible was to have him diagnosed now so he could start his early intervention therapies. I thought to myself, What are these people not understanding? A year was unacceptably too long to wait—time was running out.

I spent my days hustling to figure out how to outsmart the system. I thought, I'll call the doctor's office every week until the receptionist gets sick of me. I'll drive them crazy and they will bump us up on the list just to avoid my weekly phone call. In the meantime though, Kunal and I did research, attended conferences, and reached out to anyone we thought could help. We have a friend who is a pediatrician in Texas and we called her up to ask for her advice. In our conversation, I said to her, "You don't understand—I am so desperate to figure things out for my son that I would prostitute myself if it meant getting him what he needs." That's the level of anguish I was feeling.

Meanwhile, Kunal had unlocked the loophole. At a conference, he learned that there was a lesser known doctor at the Hôpital Notre-Dame who was able to diagnose autism. We got lucky, and within three months we had our appointment.

I have to confess that by the time Keyan was "officially" diagnosed, we already knew he was autistic. It was killing me to have the confirmation. There were times when I thought, For sure this child is autistic, and other times when I doubted it. I remember thinking he was so jealous of Manisha that he would push her away when I was holding him. I thought it was cute that he didn't want to share his mama. It was most likely her presence in his bubble. Day in and day out, I was making myself crazy trying to find evidence that Keyan wasn't autistic, so I hired a private psychologist who came to our house to observe our son and ask us a plethora of questions. After three hours she was convinced that Keyan was on the spectrum. Why did we then go to the hospital? Because in Quebec, at the time, a true diagnosis could only be issued by a neuro-psychologist (not just any psychologist).

All I ever wanted to be was a mom. I dreamed of having four children who would one day bless me with too many grandchildren to count. The recurring dream I had for my life was this: sitting in a rocking chair beside Kunal in our old age on a sun-filled day, watching our children and grandchildren run around on a lush patch of grass, chasing each other, laughing and having fun. Giggles filling the air. There are too many people to count, but all I can think is, Wow, all of these people are mine. These people were born or came together because of the life Kunal and I created.

On June 27, 2005, at the age of twenty months, my beautiful, curly-haired baby boy was formally diagnosed with autism. The dreams I had for my life were drastically altered. It felt as though my world was turned upside down, and the wish I had for my two children to be valuable contributors to society was threatened. I feared the diagnosis would have negative impacts for both of my kids. I didn't know how, but I just knew it made our family different from others. Both my husband and I would grieve in our own unique ways. His son might never be able to participate in the sports he loved, and I would never hear my son say, "Mommy, I love you." We would only learn the magnitude of Keyan's autism as he aged. Certain milestones that were never reached pertained to language. We had to reconcile that the life we had hoped for would never be. All we had envisioned for our son would never come to fruition.

The first few months following Keyan's diagnosis were the

hardest. We were put on a waiting list for him to receive services, and again told the average wait time was another year. As his mom, I felt hopeless because I knew early intervention was key. Research shows that treatment is most effective before five years of age when a brain is still forming, malleable, and has the most plasticity, therefore giving treatments a better chance at being effective in the long term. Early interventions not only give children the best start possible, but also the best chance of developing to their full potential. Therefore, the sooner a child gets help, the greater the chance for learning and progress. I refused to accept what was happening to my son. The fact that he was being denied his basic human rights—in this case access to therapy—by the Quebec government didn't sit well with me, and this is where my advocacy journey begins.

As Keyan's mom, I wasn't going to wait around for the Quebec health care system to take care of my child. I took matters into my own hands. While waiting for the public system to provide Keyan with services, we spent an estimated $30,000 in therapies the first year following his diagnosis. The list of therapies and specialists included: psychologists, applied behavioural analysis therapy, speech therapy, occupational therapy, special foods (gluten-free/casein-free diet), vitamins, and Defeat Autism Now (DAN) doctor consultations/testing. My husband and I were convinced we were going to "fix" our son—there is a mass of literature on the internet—poisonous rhetoric—that claims it can be done. Obviously, the $30,000 a year was not a sustainable plan. Eventually, it would put us in financial ruin. I set out to knock down every door and bully my way into getting my son the services the government owed him, and I finally succeeded. It is a well known fact that the government may provide services, but they are rarely adequate or enough. I told myself that once my son was taken care of, I would go about helping other families faced with the same horrible reality of waiting to have their child diagnosed or to receive essential services.

We were ready, willing, and able to do anything to give our son all of the tools he needed to bring him as close to normal as possible, because we thought that was what we were supposed to do. Our focus shifted from wanting more children to taking care of the two we already had. Getting Keyan all the help he needed became my mission. It was my full time job, all the while praying that I could be a good enough mom to Manisha by providing her love and support too. She needed to know that she was equally important to her "special needs" brother. I have heard horror stories of how the neurotypical sibling(s) can get tossed aside, and then grow to resent their "special needs" sibling because of all the attention they get. I was hyper-aware and determined not to make that mistake.

We knew we had to make a final decision on whether or not to have more children. We consulted the top doctor in autism at the Royal Victoria Hospital in Montreal to discuss the probability of having another child on the spectrum. If he had said there was no chance, I would have left there wanting to get pregnant immediately. That is how badly I wanted a large family. He explained that autism research was pointing in the direction of autism being a genetic disorder, magnified by environmental factors. We had a one in five chance of having another child with autism. It was a risk we were not willing to take.

As time went on, it was obvious that Keyan had more than autism. We would come to discover that he, like many children with an autism spectrum disorder (ASD), had what I call a "grocery list" of other coexisting conditions, referred to as comorbidities. In addition to autism, Keyan has attention deficit disorder (ADD), intellectual delays, generalized anxiety, and a sleep disorder. His ADD made it very hard for him to learn new things because he couldn't focus and sit for long enough to learn. Despite his slow learning curve (I always said he learned at a snail's pace backwards) we have been committed to staying the course, which is to provide him with all of the tools necessary to learn, live, and grow. It was the only way we could go to bed at peace each night—knowing we were doing absolutely everything we could for our little boy.

Thinking about all of the efforts we were making, I said to my husband, "There has got to be more to our story—something bigger—let's hope something even amazing."

Lost Hope

Over the course of the years, it was becoming apparent that the one thing I wanted most for my son would not come to pass. Keyan was not acquiring language. This automatically meant that my strong desire for him to integrate into a regular school would be impossible. This was another wave of grief I had to process. All of my praying didn't work. There would be several periods of great pain, sadness, and darkness. Imagine your child never being able to tell you stories about their day, how they are feeling, or what their heart most desires—their hopes and dreams.

By the age of four, having worked closely with a speech therapist, I was told that my son would never speak. Totally devastated, I went about writing an email to her manager explaining that never under any circumstances should a therapist remove hope from parents. This highlighted the inadequacies of those working in the government system. It was never part of her job to break that news. In spite of everything, I held onto hope, having read that some autistic children only start speaking as late as six, seven, or eight years old. I was so mad at her. She was part of the team. She was supposed to be rooting for Keyan's success, rather than tearing it down. I was so hurt and angry.

The beginning of any autism journey is the worst. It is riddled with doubt, pain, and grief. There is no magical team that swoops in to save your child, marriage, or family. There is not even a survival guide. It is a labyrinth of figuring out this shit as you go.

I remained hopeful that he might speak until he turned ten years old. Then I gave up. I had to let go of hope.

Parents to "Normal" Kids

As Kunal and I bear witness to other children reaching their milestones, we are constantly reminded of the ones Keyan will never reach: first sentence, high school graduation, athletic endeavours, first job, girlfriend, degree, first apartment, career, wedding, baby—the list goes on. As parents, we have to hold onto hope for our children and their future—that's our job right? Some people think I'm being a pessimist. The truth is, our reality makes people uncomfortable. Pointing out what an individual will never be able to do is daunting, and so most people respond by saying things like, "You never know." I am a realist, not a pessimist, and I f***ing know my son's limitations. Keyan will live his whole life depending on us and others; he will never graduate, marry, or have a first kiss. Only his father, sister, and I will love him unconditionally. I am not saying this to make anyone uncomfortable. I am saying it because these are the facts of our lives.

Every time I am part of your children's recitals, graduations, and weddings, don't tell me, "You never know." When I attend any kind of special event, I survive another death. The heartbreak is real. I don't want to make you feel bad or uncomfortable by telling you this. It's important for me that you know what I am going through despite the smile on my face. Every time you say to me, "You never know," you are denying my reality and painting another life which is not mine. As you say those words to me, I die yet another death.

Why do I say death? The pain associated with what my son will never do is worse than what I can describe in words. I wish I had the vocabulary or wizardry of words to paint an accurate portrait for you. But it's an impossible task. The life you have with your normally developing children makes it close to impossible for you to empathize with me. You can pretend to know, but I am sorry: you don't know the real pain, heart break, frustrations, stress, disappointment, and suffering of it all. I need to tell you that parents to children on the spectrum suffer. We may not want to show you all the suffering, but it exists, it is intense, and it is very real.

When we grieve, it is a very lonely process. We have to learn to deal with the pain in order to go on. Yet when someone dies they die once and with time we learn to live without them. Grief makes it hard to see that with time we will move forward. We never forget the ones we lose because they live within the fabric of our souls. Even years after they have departed, we may find ourselves crying, yearning to be with them one more time. One more hug, kiss, or laugh—another millisecond of togetherness. While the grief never truly goes away, the intensity of it fades. Having a child with autism or any other severe disability means that there is a constant of grieving.

While our children live life—in their limited capacity—

while simultaneously watching yours live out their full potential—it is in those instances that our hearts break. Please acknowledge our experience and give us the space, patience, and grace we need to survive yet another death.

Raising Two

Manisha is older than Keyan by seventeen months. After Keyan was born, I had to manage two babies alone. It was an incredibly overwhelming time for me. I wanted to be that supermom, so I put an extreme amount of pressure on myself. I kept Manisha in day care to maintain my sanity and to spend time alone bonding with Keyan. She liked day care so I didn't feel guilty about it.

When she was little she liked to dance and draw. I thought she was right-brain dominant because she took her art seriously, drawing almost every day, as though it was her job. I have a collection of her early works and still they make me smile. To help develop her artistic side even more, we put her in drama and got her private piano lessons. Kunal and I wanted to provide her with as many opportunities as possible so she could decide where she ultimately wanted to put her energy.

As Manisha ages, it has become obvious that she is more like her papa—a "type A" personality—left brain dominant, or what I call the cerebral type. She excels in school. She loves it. Her education is her new job, and unfortunately the arts got tossed aside. I think she may be left-brain dominant but she also has a lot of right-brain qualities: her genuine love of music and comedy.

I always felt there were two things that I needed to instil in Manisha. One was a healthy self-esteem, and the other was a focus on being a well-rounded individual. Having been a teenage girl myself, I know many issues arise from having low self-esteem. I thought that if I continually ensured that she felt safe, loved, respected, and heard here at home, then it would garner a healthy sense of self. To foster a well-rounded development, we encouraged her to try many things. In high school, she would join the volleyball team and get involved in organizing committees.

We focused a lot on Manisha's wellbeing. We never wanted her to feel *less than* because she has an autistic brother. Sometimes people are cruel or jealous and will use what is perceived as weakness to get to you. Bullies will use any kind of ammunition to break you down. From an early age, I had hard conversations with her concerning Keyan. My goal was to provide her ammunition to fight back or at least grow a "thick skin" to protect herself. Manisha rarely came home with stories of people degrading her, her brother, or her family. Part of me knows she held back from telling me things because she didn't want to hurt my feelings. Manisha protected me. There were a few times that close friends or teachers let me know of incidents that she chose not to tell me about. When I confronted her with things that I had heard, my main concern was always to ensure that she was okay. If she was open to it, we would discuss things further, but if she needed to shut it down, I respected that too.

I don't claim to fully understand the scope of Manisha's

reality as Keyan's sister, but she has provided incredible insight with a slam poem that she wrote in her grade seven English class. She would later go on to read her poem to a room of four hundred people at an S.Au.S. gala event. It would be a standing ovation with not a dry eye in the house.

Manisha's Slam Poem

How to describe my brother—special.
Some people call it autism.
But before you judge him,
learn to love him.
Because there are not tantrums every five minutes
and there are not hurricanes who destroy everything in
their path.
But when he opens his mouth to speak,
all that comes out is:
air.
If you met my five-year-old self I'd explain it like this:
he can't have a conversation like you and me
but he can express himself,
just differently.
Instead of speaking
he'll yell.
Instead of saying, "I love you,"
he'll touch my nose.
Instead of being the definition of normal,
he is the definition of different.
But different isn't bad,
different is not humiliating,

different isn't dangerous.
But most people are brought up to fear the unknown,
to most people my brother is that unknown.
And I try to explain it in a million different ways
but some people can't comprehend when
all I am trying to say is,
he is human.
But unlike you and me he doesn't care what people think about him.
He doesn't care about all the stares
in the grocery store when he is yelling and all he is
trying to do is speak.
He doesn't care about the little kids asking their parents about him
as we go to the park.
He doesn't care about all the stares constantly glued to his back.
He doesn't care.
He cares about three things:
1) his family
2) his teachers and babysitters who take care of him
3) food
How cool would it be to not care?
But I care.
I care that my parents will never hear their son say, "I love you,"
so, I repeat it more than I mean it
to spare their pain.
I care that I always see people fighting for freedom of speech,
but I have never seen anyone fight for those who can't speak.
I care that when my parents are gone, he will be my responsibility and he is a
weight I will never be able to lift off my shoulders.

I care that I will never have a fight with my brother and every day I hear my friends complaining about their siblings.
I can care all I want but I know worrying will only make it worse.
I care but I also wonder.
I wonder what goes through his mind during the day,
what pictures his mind paints,
what the voice inside his mind tells him.
I wonder if he knows he is special in his own beautiful way.
I wonder if he thinks I am a good sister who takes care of him.
I wonder if he knows what a sister is.
I can wonder all I want but I know I will never obtain the answers.
But I do know this,
he is my brother and I love him to bits and pieces
and I am proud of him.
My brother has the warmest soul, which is full of happiness and joy.
His love takes years to obtain it but once you have received it,
it is unconditional.
He is like a teddy bear,
his hugs last forever but there's not one moment during them that I feel less loved.
His smile is contagious—it could spread across the room like wildfire.
His laugh makes me smile because his joy is mine.
He lights up the lives of many
just by:
a laugh,
a hug, a smile.
All without words.
He proves that a smile is worth a thousand words,

and if my brother can do that,
he could change the world.

*I posted the video of her reciting her poem on Facebook and YouTube and it got over twenty-five thousand views combined. It still gives me goose bumps and makes me cry.

Little Teachers

It's crazy how we have the capacity to love unconditionally. The happiest day of my life was when Manisha was born because it finally made me a mother, something I had longed to be. After two and a half years of infertility treatments and a miscarriage, I was finally a mom. When they put her on my chest our eyes met and I was overcome with a love I had never known.

Keyan's birth story was very different. Labouring him was a traumatic experience. It was a struggle to get his ten pound body through the birth canal. We learned that the problem was shoulder dystocia. Also known as birth trauma, this condition happens when one or both of the baby's shoulders get stuck in the birth canal, and it can be dangerous for both mother and baby. Both my children's birth stories are similar in that they both had shoulder dystocia, but Keyan's size meant that he was stuck for longer in the birth canal.

The day after I gave birth, Kunal brought the staff Krispy Kreme doughnuts as a thank you. They proceeded to tell him that they were extremely nervous during Keyan's birth because it was so hard to get him out. I had in fact registered the fear on their faces while birthing Keyan, but I had to ignore them to get through it. I had begged the doctor to C-section him out but she told me it was too late. I was suffering so badly that I hated my doctor at that moment. By the time I had to push for Keyan, there was little to no epidural left. When he was finally born I was utterly exhausted; he was taken to be evaluated and so my baby boy and I never had that bonding moment like I did with Manisha. I guess it was the earliest sign that being Keyan's mom would never be easy.

In the wee hours of October 1, 2003, my greatest teacher, Keyan Nalik Saha, came into my life and changed it forever. Our greatest teachers are those that make us question everything and strip us to the core of our being. They show us parts of ourselves we didn't know were there. On far too many occasions to count, Keyan has brought me to my knees begging, crying, and praying to a higher power to figure out how to live with the stress, the frustration, and the cruel reality of raising an autistic child. Times get so dark that I fear we, as a family, may stay stuck—helpless, hopeless, fearful, and alone.

As a mama bear, I can't wallow. Instead, I forage for anything that will bring us back to light, love, and happiness. In times of desperation I go back to basics—to the things about Keyan that make this journey special, unique, and worth living. Don't get me wrong; there are moments that bring us tremendous happiness. In those moments, it feels as though our hearts will explode. This is where Keyan has taught us the most valuable lessons of all: life is all about the small stuff.

"The best and most beautiful
things in the world cannot be seen
or even touched
—they must be felt with the heart."

-Helen Keller

Les Lilas Society

My activism became important to me. I thought that the more I told my story, the better people would understand the complexities of raising a child like Keyan. I also wanted people to see that life could be lived outside of being his mom. As a woman, I had my own goals and dreams to fulfil.

As stated on the "About" page of their website, "Les Lilas Society is a platform for everyday people to practice using their voice and find meaning in their story." It was founded by two Montreal friends with the goal of connecting people to story. I was invited to be a speaker at one of their events. I stood on stage in a room filled with close to one hundred women and I shared my story. I worked hard on delivering something that I hoped would be inspiring. The talk I gave that evening echoes throughout this book. It is a kind of highlight reel of the past fifteen years of my life.

Les Lilas–Running

In order to cope with the reality of having a son with
severe autism
I decided I needed to do something for myself
because I was on the verge of a nervous breakdown.
Daily I would experience generalized anxiety and
sometimes suffer from panic attacks.
There were moments when I couldn't breathe.
I thought if only I could run away from my life.
BUT I couldn't run
because I loved my husband and children.
Then I thought if only I could escape the chaos for a while.
I desperately needed to find a coping mechanism.

It happened suddenly.
I picked up a pair of running shoes and headed out the
door.
I ran and I ran and I ran.
I felt like Forrest Gump although I wasn't running, I wasn't
even jogging but I was shuffling forward.
I don't think my feet really left the pavement.
Although it was hard I felt free—
no one depending on me—

no one bothering me—
no tantrums—
no expectations—
I was not a mom, wife, daughter, or friend.
At that moment I was just Audrey.

At the time I had no fancy watch so I had no idea how far
I had run.
All I knew is that when I left the house and looked at the
clock and again upon my return
forty-five minutes had passed.
The next day, anxious to find out how far I had travelled
I drove my car along the route.
I had managed to run five kilometers.
I was super proud of myself!!!
It gave me a sense of accomplishment.
Even more important than that
is that I felt FREE—
I came home lighter and more focused.
I felt some of the anxiety diminish.
Over time running became a PASSION I wasn't expecting.
I couldn't wait to run again
And that's because every time I did
I felt more alive and less stressed.
THEN
I started to challenge myself—
Push myself.
My first official race was a 10k.
On race day I discovered another amazing feeling.
It was incredible to be surrounded by positive energy.
A total BUZZ of enthusiasm
—like minded people gathered together to RUN.
I was hooked!!!
I loved everything about running
—the highs and lows

—the questions and the answers
—(eventually) the competitiveness with self
and competitiveness with others.
Running helped me stave off the stress of raising Keyan
—I shared my running journey on social media and
oftentimes people would message me telling me that I
was inspiring.
I would negate by saying
I only run because if I didn't run
I would be chasing down pills with a bottle of wine.
I knew running was good for my brain
—it kept me steady and minimized potential depression
(not to say I haven't had my moments despite running).

Why I Learned to Run

The idea for running first came about because of a pact I made with some other ladies one night in my garage over cigarettes and wine. As a sedentary mom of two I thought that running a ten kilometer race was a big deal, but what started out as a mere bet turned out instead to be the beginning of a beautiful journey for me. Running would become a metaphor for my life.

Running should be easy—right? After all, our ancestors ran all over the place. But our egos tend to get in the way. We tie up our laces and sprint out the door. After one city block our lungs expand in agony and our minds scream, thinking, Holy shit I can't do this. How the hell do people do this? What was I thinking? An even bigger question is, how do people actually enjoy this?

I knew when I started training for the ten kilometer race that if I sprinted out the door it was a sure way to jeopardize any hope of success. Instead, I went slow and steady. It wasn't so much a run but rather a forward-moving shuffle. I remember that day so well. There was an older man in front of me—he served as my personal pace bunny—albeit back then I had no clue what a pace bunny was. When I reached home I felt so accomplished. I had checked the clock when I left the house and I checked it again upon my return. That was the accuracy of my timing when I started out in 2007. The only technology I relied on in the beginning was my MP3 player. I desperately needed music to distract me. The music helped to drown out the negativity. I got lost in song.

Every time I put on my shoes, my goal is to run longer. The next time I laced up I set out to run for forty-six minutes, then forty-seven minutes, then forty-eight minutes, etc. Speed was not my focus, but time was. I wanted to be away from my chaotic life for as long as I could. In the beginning of my running journey I ran three days a week. I was never athletic and was grossly out of shape. My motivator wasn't to become a big runner, but merely to use running as an excuse to get out of the house, to be away from the constant calls for mommy (from Keyan it came in high pitched screams). Being alone with my own thoughts without distractions felt like a vacation. I felt free, and that became my second motivation for running. While training to win "the bet," which was to run ten kilometers, I discovered more than running. I found myself again. The "me" time—my newfound time alone— helped me reconnect with the parts of me that I had lost. When I ran I wasn't a wife, mother, or friend—I was simply me, Audrey.

When choosing which ten kilometer race to run, I didn't overthink it. I settled on the closest race to home which happened to be the Terry Fox Run in Saint-Lambert. It was a fundraiser and I did my part by collecting and donating four hundred dollars for the charity. It was a fun run rather than a race, but I didn't even know the difference at the time. I remember it being a perfect fall day—sunny and not too hot or cold. Kunal came along with the kids. I was surprised to see that most in attendance were families who were there to walk around the track a few times. I believe there were only three of us committed to running the ten kilometers. It turned out to be a ten kilometer run in several loops that circled the park. No clocks, no timing chips, and no spectators—or so I thought.

To my surprise, as I was running, I saw people gathering around my family and it turned out to be my best friend Chriss along with her son, Nate. They had come all the way from Ottawa. Then there were others. My dear friends Shena and Bernie, along with their kids, and also Kim and Rob with their two boys. My therapist at the time showed up with her elderly father to applaud my efforts, too. Sadly, they were the only spectators in the park, but they were all there cheering me on. I sucked back my tears because it is extremely hard to run and cry at the same time. I was overwhelmed with their show of support to come see me so early on a Sunday morning.

Despite not having the usual pomp and circumstance of a big city race, I can attest to the fact that what I experienced was incredibly special. Surrounded by love, I completed my first ten kilometer race. No podium, no medal, but a heart filled with love and pride.

In the photos from that day, my kiddies wore awesome orange T-shirts that my best friend made for them to wear. I also see evidence of things done à la "Odd-rey"—perfectly imperfect. So many things were off, weird, and different than what a race usually is, but that represents so much of who I am—a woman jumping in with two feet before even feeling the water.

Birth of an Organization

Who am I? I am a woman, wife, mother, friend, runner, and advocate. Of all the titles assigned to me, the most important is the role of "mom." Before having children, I vowed to myself that I would be the best mom I could be, and that meant raising children who felt loved, protected, valued, heard, and supported throughout their lives. Becoming a mother naturally made me want to be a better person, but becoming a mom to a boy with autism forced me to be the best human being I could be. It didn't take long after Keyan's diagnosis for me to realize that life for him and our family would be a steady uphill battle against peers, family, friends, the government, the health care system, the educational system, and even at times ourselves. Once I had a clear picture of my son's limitations and his future as a non-verbal individual, I started to call myself "the voice for the voiceless." I needed to be Keyan's voice, advocate, protector, ears, and biggest cheerleader, and if I was going to be all those things for my son then I thought, Why not for others too?

Around the time of the diagnosis I was working in a high school as a substitute teacher. I loved my job, the people I worked with, and especially the students! I needed these people to see me—to understand me and my reality. I spoke openly of my son's autism in the hope that it would make people more comfortable with it. I thought, If we could bring people together to talk about autism, to learn more about it, and to ask them to be a part of it (in terms of support) then I was convinced it would make my life easier. I would feel less alone—less isolated.

In 2009 while at work at Heritage Regional High School I had an "aha" moment. This was a few years after I had discovered running and fallen in love with the sport. I realized that at my disposal was a large pool of manpower. By that point, I had participated in several charity runs and I loved the atmosphere. Running for charity wasn't simply about running at a certain pace, it was about helping others. Combine those things together, and I thought, Aha, I could organize an awareness run for autism.

One day while in a science lab I decided to write a letter to my city asking permission to host a five kilometer event on the streets of Candiac. It was my students who gave me the courage to actually write it. Before turning to my computer I asked them this question. "If I were to host a five kilometer event for Autism Awareness Month—would you come out to volunteer? It would mean you would have to get up incredibly early on a Sunday morning. I mean like 6 or 7 a.m.! Would you do that?" The response was a resounding yes. I quickly learned to embrace the old adage, "Ask and you shall receive," and asked my colleagues, my family, my friends, my neighbours, and my community to join us.

In April of 2009, we all came together for what I named the first "Autism Awareness Run/Walk" to be held in my city. I didn't know what I was doing but I jumped in with my two feet and took a leap of faith. I was not going to be alone in this battle. I was desperate to ensure my family did not become isolated from society. I rushed to put together a group of my friends to form a committee. We had 225 participants walk/run as a show of support. I had seventy-five students come out that day to volunteer. The inaugural event was deemed a success. The message about needing love, acceptance, and support was spread.

The following year, the Autism Awareness Run/Walk collected $6000 from the adult participants. I felt a great deal of responsibility to spend it as fast as possible. I hustled to decide what to do with the money we had raised. Autism was draining due to all the doctor, psychologist, and therapist visits. As a family we were exhausted— instead of bringing our children to activities, our lives revolved around autism. One day while I was bringing Manisha to ballet class at the local community center, it hit me hard. *The injustice of special needs children being left out.* "Discarded" is the word that best describes how it feels to a parent. While my heart was full for my daughter, it equally broke for my son. I thought all children, regardless of their circumstance, should have access to sports, leisure, and fun. All children should be granted the opportunity to play and be around their peers. It seemed so unfair. Not only was my son limited by the brain he was born with, but he was also limited by society. This was the beginning of my life's work—my purpose.

Keyan had been enjoying one-on-one music therapy for quite some time, so it felt like a natural place for me to start. I solicited Keyan's music therapist to run a class supported by two other adults to shadow the participants. That fall, I put together a twelve week music therapy program in a rented space at the community center. It accommodated eight eager participants. I became the self-titled "programs coordinator." We were on our way, with no manual to follow, and making it all up as we went along. The next year, I was able to add more programs to the roster. The programs were meant to provide autistic kids a life outside of home and school. I wanted to build programs that provided a safe environment for the kids, where they would be surrounded by people who understood their uniqueness and who would nurture them, rather than expect them to be something they weren't.

What started off as a fundraising run comprised of volunteers and operating out of my basement, had turned into a full blown organization, Soutien Autism Support (S.Au.S.). It is complete with a board of directors, organizing committees, program coordinator, office employees, an office space rental, teachers, shadows, and over a hundred volunteers a year. All of this was spawned by the fear of children being left out, and the overwhelming love a mother has for her children. I added to the list of my roles: I was now and would always be the founder of a charitable organization. It takes a village to raise a child but it takes an army to raise a child like Keyan.

Humble Beginnings

I have to admit I did things backwards. Usually people start by sourcing funding before starting a project or creating a business plan. Not me! When I decided to organize the Autism Awareness Run, I was operating on a zero-dollar budget. As a family, we spent every last dollar on our son's therapy and we started to feel the financial stress. I hadn't made a business plan and had no idea what I was doing but it was bigger than me. I had to do this. The 2010 edition of the Autism Awareness Run was the first time I attempted to raise money for the cause. I knew firsthand that there wasn't an organization on the South Shore of Montreal that was worthy of the money I raised. I did what I thought was best to use the money to build programs. Everything blossomed from there.

I was in charge of the day to day operations for the first five years of the existence of S.Au.S. By myself, I ran things out of an office in the basement of my house. My friends generously gave of their time to ensure the success of the run, but there was more to it for S.Au.S. I was responsible for the administrative tasks along with the running of the programs. For a while, I was high on the success, but as the number of programs increased, I began to feel worn down.

I often questioned the organization's sustainability as I had structured it, where volunteers would help for three months out of the year. I couldn't keep going like this, so I had to figure out how to move forward in a way that would keep me healthy and sane. I yearned for success and longevity if I was going to help people. I made the decision to hire someone to help me with the operations. It was the step that freed up some of my time so that I could build upon and improve our programs. Eventually, I would need to hire a programs coordinator to do that work so I could focus on growth. As the founder and visionary of S.Au.S. I have to admit I had many ideas, but I learned to contain myself in order to ensure that we provided top quality services for our participants. I believed in laying a solid foundation before moving forward, and I can confidently say that with this philosophy, we have successfully built a solid organization. The standards of practice that I live by is to make sure that no one gets left behind. We need to make space for families that look different than what is considered normal. I successfully did that with S.Au.S.

A Family Affair

My husband of twenty-five years had supported me throughout my time at S.Au.S. From the very beginning, he wanted to see me succeed. He was always willing to roll up his sleeves to help. Over the years, he volunteered hundreds of hours. The first thing he did was to help craft the flyer for that first Autism Awareness Run/Walk with the iconic illustration of a boy with three fingers. Over the years, the boy morphed into something more sophisticated that included life-like hands. The boy became symbolic—it was as though when the organization grew, the boy grew too, serving as a visual reminder of our success. The boy was taken from stock images on the internet, and was later enhanced with the help of graphic designers. Kunal was always willing to give his advice and opinion on things. When we were struggling to name the organization, it was Kunal who came up with Soutien-Autism(e)-Support. He also offered his time by keeping the books in order, setting up events, and taking them down. This caused tension in our marriage, because we both wanted to do things our own way. It was my work, and I wanted him to be more supportive of my vision, but he was insistent that he knew better. I absolutely hate it when people tell me what to do, and I felt he was always telling me what I should be doing. When the organization had enough money, I hired an office assistant so I could do things independently of Kunal. I needed him out of things in order to keep my marriage. This is something I never talked about with anyone. It was difficult for us to work together, but at first we had no choice because the organization had no money. We did the best we could, but it caused lots of friction in the home—particularly when it was crunch time for the Autism Awareness Run, which is held in April during Autism Awareness Month.

Manisha also played a large role in my work. When she was little, she walked the Autism Awareness Run with family, and when she got old enough, she volunteered to help. The morning of the run she would help set up, work her volunteer post, and then help with the take down. When I would go to her high school to recruit volunteers, she would encourage her classmates to sign up. It was the same with the gala we hosted in the fall when a bunch of her classmates would offer to help us set up. I tried as hard as possible to make it fun for these kids so they would come back year after year, and they did! All of the students who volunteered were amazing, and every year the adults at the run would tell me so. Manisha was also a huge support at home, making sure Keyan was well taken care of in my absence.

All we had hoped for year after year is that Keyan would show up to the Autism Awareness Run and walk with Kunal and his service dog, Bagou. The first few years, when Keyan was little, it was easier because he was pulled in a little red wagon. It seemed as though the wagon was his safe place, but once he outgrew it things got harder. I stressed more about how Kunal and Keyan were faring, rather than actually hosting the event. When the weather was cold, I hoped that Kunal had all the proper gear to make Keyan comfortable, including warm clothes and snacks. Kunal always handled things like a rock star! Over the years, things improved and they were able to stay much longer to enjoy the post-run offerings. In the last few years, Kunal even kept track of how long it would take the three of them to walk the five kilometer course. The first time they completed it I was at the finish line waiting to medal my son.

Les Lilas–A Huge Dream

Recently I have been reading "The School of Greatness" by Lewis Howes.
Lewis interviews Kyle Maynard
who was born with underdeveloped limbs
—his arms end at his elbows
and his legs above the knee.
This man went on to be a world renowned speaker.
He used to cry himself to sleep as a little boy wishing he had limbs.
Despite that he still participated in athletic endeavours.
At eleven years old he made his first tackle and his life changed at that moment.
Do you know why?
Because in that moment he went from worrying and wishing about his future.
"It was in that action and the perseverance in the face of tall odds that obstacles started to dissolve and he took his first concrete steps toward greatness" (Lewis Howes, The School of Greatness (Rodale, 2015), 34.
This is where I can draw parallels.
I didn't know what I was doing when I started the Autism Awareness Run

—I just went for it
—I made my first tackle.
What I wanted out of that was to feel less alone
—for people to understand autism
—accept my son
—and others just like him.
I feared being alone
my family being ostracized.
That was the catalyst for it all.
It didn't start with a huge DREAM of creating an organization.
It was all born out of wanting my son to be accepted for who he is.
My family to be accepted for what we looked like—
DIFFERENT NOT LESS.

What happened was when I obtained one goal I created another.
What started off as an awareness run
—turned into a fundraiser that
—then created programs for children with autism
—that then turned into a non-profit organization
—then I had to hire office staff
—rent an office space
—create more programs
—became a charitable organization
—that grew in the number of participants
—the number of programs
—from helping children to helping teens too.

With every passing year S.Au.S. was growing to reach more people and provide more programs, making S.Au.S. a pillar of the autism community. This was no longer a small grassroots organization born of my desire to make a change; it had become federally and provincially recognized. I was the head of a successful organization that made a real difference by helping hundreds of families on a yearly basis.

How Do You Do It?

People often ask me, how do you do it? Too shy to ask them to elaborate on the question, I assume they mean, how do I find the stamina to care for a special needs child, work, head a community organization, and run all at the same time? The answer is I don't do it alone. I have an incredibly supportive husband. Throughout our many years together, Kunal has always wanted me to find fulfilment in my life. If that meant going back to work after the children were born, training for a marathon, or hosting an event, he was right there with me. It is not to say there hasn't been resistance on his part, but he knows when I have something in my head that I am going to see it through.

Being married to a good husband-turned-father has been key to many of my personal accomplishments. Let's start with caring for a special needs child. I truly believe my kids won the dad lottery! He is extremely dedicated to their health, happiness, and future. When the kids were young and Kunal was working hard to climb the corporate ladder, he never used that as an excuse to bow out of fatherly duties. Every night after work he would change out of his suit and into something more comfortable and then proceed to roll up his sleeves—he would get on the floor to play with the kids, help feed them at supper time, and participate in the bedtime routine. Oftentimes I thought Kunal was a better parent than me.

I thought I wanted to be a full time stay-at-home mother, but it got lonely. I yearned for adult conversation. Before Manisha's first birthday, I decided to put my name in as a substitute teacher. I got a call the very next day. What I loved about my job was the flexibility to say yes or no to work. The school's receptionist would call me in the morning and I could accept or refuse to work that day. It meant I could be there for Manisha when she needed me. It was the perfect work-home balance. I loved the job. I managed working part-time at school and part-time building the organization. This was also the time when I was discovering the benefits of running. All of this was happening at once, but I was able to strike the perfect balance between caring for my family, myself, and others. I learned that living in service to others was an incredibly enriching experience. It actually energized me to be building programs and helping families. Things were manageable because I had control over my schedule. I was happy and fulfilled in many ways.

How do you do it?

I don't mind answering candid questions. In fact, ask me anything you like. Because I would rather you ask anything rather than make false assumptions. I remember a teacher once asked me how I was able to walk through the halls with a smile on my face. What she was really asking me was how I could be so happy while having the burden of caring for a child with special needs. I told her, "If this is my one precious life, then I am going to make the best of it." In essence, my special needs son Keyan would never be my excuse.

I am confronted by the questions, "Who do I think I am?" or "Am I good enough to do this work and be the voice for the voiceless?" I have no experience in running a non-profit organization. Then again, I had no experience hosting a major sporting event either. Negative thoughts crept into my consciousness, and then I realized that no one else seemed to care enough to do the work. So I looked for mentors to help me push through and to help change my negative self-talk. I discovered Brené Brown's TED Talk on YouTube (YouTube; "Brené Brown: Why Your Critics Aren't The Ones Who Count," by Brené Brown, Dec 4, 2013) and she refers to this beautiful quote:

"It is not the critic who counts; not the man who points out how the strong man stumbles, or where the doer of deeds could have done them better. The credit belongs to the man who is actually in the arena, whose face is marred by dust and sweat and blood; who strives valiantly; who errs, who comes short again and again, because there is no effort without error and shortcoming; but who does actually strive to do the deeds; who knows great enthusiasms, the great devotions; who spends himself in a worthy cause; who at the best knows in the end the triumph of high achievement, and who at the worst, if he fails while daring greatly, so that his place shall never be with those cold and timid souls who neither know victory nor defeat."

(The Man in the Arena, delivered at the Sorbonne, Paris on April 23, 1910)
-*Theodore Roosevelt*

A Word to the Next Generation

One of the things I loved most about my work at S.Au.S. was the awareness campaign. I would go to schools and give talks about autism. My goal was to educate as many students, teachers, and staff as possible, providing them a firsthand account of what it is like to raise a person like Keyan. I would often first define autism and then talk about Keyan's diagnosis, his limitations, how it felt to be his parent, how I discovered running, and ultimately the work being done at S.Au.S.

This is also how I recruited volunteers to come out to help with the Autism Awareness Run. Since I did these talks in April during Autism Awareness Month, it was easier to recruit. I particularly loved going back into the schools after I had left my job as a substitute teacher. I missed the students so much. My hope was to inspire students to be more compassionate towards difference.

These talks could go either way. Either I left feeling elated that the talk was a success or I left completely demoralized by the students' responses. Believe it or not, there were times when teachers had to remove students for snide remarks. Once I felt so attacked I lost my train of thought and it took me a good ten minutes to compose myself. The students were none the wiser because I continued my talk, but my thoughts were jumbled. Things were not coming out as smoothly as usual.

I get it, though. Some kids have no filter, yearn for attention of any kind, or find the topic uncomfortable. I remember being a kid and growing up with little to no education on how to approach people with disabilities. I remember seeing them as "other," almost as if there was a divide and no way to bridge that gap. I was intimidated by people who were different because I wasn't taught about their humanness. That is why I visit schools. Going to schools to talk openly about my son's autism is a way to provide that necessary education. A Google search can explain autism; having a person in front of you telling you how best to approach their child provides the humanness that I was missing in order to understand difference. It is not only students that I have spent my energy on educating, but my peers as well.

Following one of my talks at a local high school, it was brought to my attention that a small group of students had created an Instagram account that was meant to degrade their fellow autistic classmates. It was cyberbullying at its finest. The staff struggled to get the page taken down. They had even reported it to Instagram without any success. I was shocked to hear that this was a thing—purposely taking photos and videos of students who are struggling—all to get a laugh or gain some type of sick notoriety. It actually made me sick. I asked if I could address the class where the suspected bullies were. I made a plea to them to take down the account and I explained why they should. By the end of the day, the page was still up. It was still up the next morning. My plea had had no effect. I decided to write an email for the principal to read to the students.

To the boys of Instagram,

When I heard the news that you had decided to create an Instagram account dedicated to making fun of your fellow students who have autism, I was flooded by anger, rage, disappointment, and genuine heartbreak. I thought, What kind of low life do you have to be to make fun of people who are born with different brains. People with autism struggle on a daily basis to fit into a world that is not made for them—there is too much noise, movement, sensation, sight, sound, smell, and emotion that overwhelm them. Every day they conquer obstacles not seen by the naked eye. It's hard for them because often they cannot articulate what they feel both physically and emotionally. It is as though their brains are bombarded by too much all at once. Their thoughts creep into the fiber of their being making their bodies feel a certain way—uncomfortable. Sensory overload often gets the better of them sending them into crisis mode. To us it looks like a tantrum but to them they are trying to release all the pent up STRESS inside.

I don't expect you to know this about people with autism unless you live or work with them. I guess I just expect common decency. That means giving every human being the respect they deserve. Your actions of creating an Instagram page in an attempt to belittle people with special needs is equivalent to racist slurs because somewhere inside, you think you are better than another group of individuals. The irony is that you have the guts to make fun of these people behind a screen where your identity is hidden. We cannot see you and that is where you are most comfortable being loud. I guess no one listens to you at home—you don't feel valued by your peers so you have to find a way to be heard even though you are hidden. So sad that you feel popular because of the number of followers that like your page who may not necessarily like what you represent but are just curious. I have one word for people like you and that is "coward." If you feel so strongly and justified with what you have to say/show then you should have the guts to say it out loud—reveal yourself.

You sit there reading/hearing this thinking Ahh—this comes from an old lady who I don't even know—who cares. What you fail to understand is that I too was a teenage kid trying to figure things out. I too was trying to make my place in this world—I too wanted to be heard. All of us adults were where you are now but we seem to have made better decisions. Instead of trying to be heard in a negative light we used our voices to make our school better; we were part of student council, we joined committees, we used our creativity to create art, if we were athletic we joined the team, and if we weren't we were cheerleaders to those who were. The sad reality is that what you decide to do will follow you; everything you do on the internet is recorded and can potentially harm your future. Look at what is going on with Facebook and Cambridge Analytica (if you don't know what I am talking about—Google it). Your past will come to haunt your future.

It's okay, we all make mistakes on this journey called life. You were not being heard and you needed to find a way. I get that. I beg you that if you want to be heard then stand up for something good. Stand up for human rights, the environment, the less fortunate, and those in need. Everyone has the potential to make positive change. I have always taught those around me that if we all took baby steps together we could do great things with our lives. Life is made up of small decisions put together rather than one grand gesture. My direction in life was sparked by being a runner and a mother to a boy with autism—it's not what I had envisioned, but it is where my life took me. I took small steps by asking people to support me and turned it little by little into a charitable organization.

I trust that although you feel that creating this Instagram page was going to be funny, you may have gotten caught up in the moment with friends and this snowballed beyond your control. What you have to realize is that it is never too late to change your mind. Think for a moment how this makes other people feel: the person you are making fun of, their families, their teachers, fellow students, and those who care. You are making fun of people who struggle but people who are very loved nonetheless. My plea to you today is to take down the sti_meme page. If you do not have the guts to come forward, I get that; simply utter the words, "I am sorry," as you delete the page. Trust me when I say the action of deleting the page will liberate you of the guilt and shame.

I take the liberty to speak on behalf of everyone by saying, "We accept your apology—we know there will be mistakes made on this journey called life but trust this was another lesson. Now go on and do good things and be kind."

A sincere thank you,
Audrey Burt
mother to Keyan
President and founder of S.Au.S.

Bubbles

We usually talk about the autistic person as living in a bubble. We rarely talk about the bubble that the family is unwittingly put into as well. Invites don't come or they eventually stop. It's not that we are not good friends—or a good time for that matter—it is because we come with a kid that makes others feel uncomfortable.

How about the sibling who is not fully comfortable having friends over? I have often wondered if Manisha altered her desires in order to avoid uncomfortable situations.

Let's talk about being in that bubble and what is on the inside and outside of it. Inside is the family unit who feels the pain of being left out and unconsidered.

The bubble makes you bury feelings that are too hard to feel. What about the countless people who come to your home and don't even acknowledge your son. You think to yourself, is it a reflection on us, him, or them? How about friends talking endlessly about their children's accomplishments, not even once considering how awful we might feel. The ugly part of me hates them for it, but then I brush it off. When I really think about it, it's sad when all people have to talk about is their children. I have a bunch of things I can talk about other than my kids.

The Beard

I never anticipated Keyan growing facial hair—it just happened. When he was as young as eight, peach fuzz emerged on the corners of his mouth. I thought, Good lord, already? I didn't realize that peach fuzz could appear so early. It definitely comes from the other side of his bloodline. I didn't think much of the peach fuzz, but everyone kept saying not to shave it too early because otherwise it would come back thicker. In all my friends' circles, cutting an immature moustache seemed a sin punishable by creating a Chewbacca-like freak. I dared not touch it.

When it comes to Keyan's appearance, Kunal and I have always been on the same page. We want our son to be clean. Clean hair, nails, and skin. We also want him to be presentable with stylish clothing. We know he will already be judged for being different, so it means a lot that we make him as attractive and approachable as possible. Keyan has always been beautiful. When he was born, he weighed a whopping nine pounds fourteen ounces. His chubby cheeks, fat thighs, and strawberry blond hair made him look cherubic. As a toddler, his hair turned curly and it added to his sweet face. Even when he went through that awkward phase of losing his teeth, he was still damn cute. When I look at Keyan as a young adult, I see the statue of David. He has the same curly hair and tall, slim, and muscular stature. I joke around with Manisha saying, "It's a good thing your brother isn't normal or else your friends would want to date him and that would suck."

Kunal is put to task. He is the one to give Keyan his first shave. Mere seconds with the electric razor removes all traces of peach fuzz. Kunal says Keyan had no hesitation. He seemed to like the vibration. It is a father's job to teach his son to shave. In this case, Keyan will not learn to shave but instead learn to be shaven. Putting the razor to Keyan's skin for the first time was because of the undeniable fact that Keyan was getting older. Kunal and I cringe at the thought, because the truth is it would be easier if Keyan stayed small, cute, and manageable. As he ages, his voice becomes deeper and sounds scary to the untrained ear. We feel the outside world grow more judgmental.

I never forecasted having to shave anyone other than myself. But I have no choice. My job as mother and caregiver is to care for Keyan in all ways. I don't get to pick and choose. It is quite the job to shave someone else, but together it is a learning curve. New patches sprout up and he learns to contort his head and neck to help me. Keyan is a mouth breather and is resistant to closing his mouth; his upper lip is never as clean shaven as I would like.

I often imagine the parents for whom shaving is a struggle. In one of our programs I had a mother report that she couldn't brush her son's teeth because he would gag. For Keyan it is impossible to cut his nails, because there is something about the sound of the clippers that drives him insane. When he was little one of us would hold him down on the bed while the other parent clipped away. We would all come out of his room red faced and drenched with sweat. Then Keyan became too big. Lucky for us, he took to biting his fingernails so that was taken care of, but we had to figure out how to deal with toenails. Eventually, he would allow us to file them.

It was in these moments that I realized that I had moved from mom to caregiver. I wasn't merely doing the usual mom stuff, I was doing what most moms never have to do.

A Mirage

The worst years with Keyan, hands down, were when he experienced a hormone shift into adolescence. Things were happening to his body that we couldn't explain to him. It was impossible to make him understand. Sitting with an overall sense of unease while experiencing growth pains and hormone shifts—without any explanation—must have been scary. This was a horrible time for Keyan, and it brought his anxiety to the forefront. Before his body started to change, I didn't realize Keyan was anxious. It was no fault of mine—in the early days I thought everything was bundled into one package labelled "autism." It was during this time that I started to realize that Keyan was dealing with more than having a neurodivergent brain.

What was helping him at school was learning at his own rhythm with an emphasis on autonomy and incorporating puzzles and games. Keyan loves puzzles and matching objects. He is competitive by nature, so he thinks that the quicker he completes a task, the better. When he plays games, he has no problems with cheating here and there. But what is most important about school for Keyan is the social aspect. It is well-documented that people thrive on human connection. Although individuals with autism prefer their own company, there are still benefits to being surrounded by others. I have always said that it is no life for a person to only be with their parents and siblings. I can't imagine a life like that for anyone. I think of it as a life within four walls, prison-like.

On occasion I see a man who looks like my son and I think, What if Keyan was neurotypical? How would he show up in the world? Who would he be? What would he do with his life? I allow myself a few moments to fantasize. I observe the individual in his likeness, laughing and smiling—radiating wholeness. I have seen versions of Keyan. One was a teenager on his skateboard, another a waiter in a restaurant, and a third a random person walking on the street texting on his phone. I know one thing for sure, had he led a normal life he would have been a super attractor. Because, like his father, the Saha male is one who makes you feel welcome, flirts just a tad, and makes you warm in their presence.

I allow myself a few minutes to get lost in my thoughts as I approach the threshold of the dark abyss and dare to ask—why him? Why us? I chase the thoughts away before I fall into the ultimate state of self-pity.

Golden Nuggets

I joke that Keyan is the centre of our universe or a Maharaja (an Indian prince). He commands much but does little. There are days when caring for Keyan is all I can do. I don't have the energy or motivation to run, cook, or tend to any other tasks really. When I have low energy days, besides meeting his needs, all I can do is flop on the sofa and binge-watch whatever I find on Netflix. When he needs me, I tend to him again. I used to feel guilty about my non-productiveness, but I have learned to let that go. I paint a portrait of how daunting it is to raise Keyan, and the truth is that it is, but living under the weight of it all would kill me so I have to look at the beauty he brings to me. Keyan brings us back to basics. He reminds us that it is humans who tend to complicate things. Here is how Keyan brings joy to our everyday:

- Keyan's smile - the one he flashes at me that reveals both the huge gaps in his teeth and the dimples which he inherited from my dad. The kind of smile that is expressed with both his mouth and his eyes. The one that says, "I love you mama," or, "Thank you mama."

- I love the fact that he doesn't care what people think of him. If he has to burp, fart, or shout out, he does what feels good to him. He is not imprisoned by expectations imposed by society. (I admit at times that this can be a challenge—but wouldn't it be great if we simply didn't give a shit what people thought of us?)

- He reminds us everyday what is important in life: family and love. He has taught his father and I that what is most important is what lives within our four walls. We are a TEAM no matter what. We have to be each other's support.

- He has taught us patience. Admittedly, I still don't have patience when it comes to stupidity, lineups, or traffic. Rather, I reserve all my patience for Keyan. I believe he deserves it most. If I lose patience with Keyan, then we all lose.

- Keyan reminds us that it's all about the simple pleasures. We get excited about the things most people take for granted:
    - A new day—starting fresh
    - A full night's sleep
    - That regardless of age my boy will always want to cuddle with his mama bear
    - Going to a restaurant and not having to rush through a meal or leave the restaurant prematurely

A Mountain of White T-shirts

One day, I decided to tackle Keyan's closet. Anyone who knows me knows that I love to organize. I love nothing more than to hunker down in a closet, get rid of things, and colour-coordinate what is left. While I was sorting through Keyan's T-shirts, I realized that, damn, he has a lot of them. But there is a reasonable explanation. First off, T-shirts are the only type of shirt option for Keyan. He cannot manipulate the buttons on a button-down shirt. He is unable to undo the buttons and ends up ripping them all off. Picture the Hulk ripping at his shirt and the front popping apart. That is Keyan in a button-down shirt. I wonder if he feels trapped, or if it's just his way to get out of the shirt. There was also a short period of time when he would chew the collar, leaving tiny bite marks. It went from bite marks to him yanking on the collar to the point of tearing the shirt completely down the middle. So, I stopped buying button-down shirts altogether. This is a great example of how we constantly have to adjust expectations to meet Keyan's needs. His learning to button and unbutton a dress shirt would be a huge victory. Never mind graduations, dates, and fast cars. As Keyan's parents, supporting him in learning to button up buttons is more aligned with our reality.

Just like with collared shirts, though, Keyan also regularly destroys T-shirts. I don't know if it started because of anxiety, or the sensory feel of it. He sometimes puts the neck band into his mouth and pulls down hard. Other times he simply chews on it, saturating it with saliva. We call him Shiva, which means "the destroyer." The problem is that Keyan tends to go through phases, and when he figured out that for whatever reason it felt good to destroy his T-shirts, there was one week where he destroyed five or six of them. Money out the window. That is why the thought of paying full price for a T-shirt and Keyan possibly destroying it after one wear doesn't make sense to me. So, I end up hitting the sales rack at Old Navy in the fall and winter to buy him a mountain of five-dollar T-shirts. Some of them make their way onto his many hangers —arranged by colour—until there is no room left for more. Some get folded up, tag left on, and stashed high up in his closet for later use.

My boy loves to eat! He does not have finesse, either. I can't begin to tell you how many shirts have fallen victim to unremovable stains. The frustrating part is that sometimes these shirts make their way back into the closet, and when I am rushing to get him ready, putting a stained shirt on him makes me absolutely crazy. It is a little thing, but it risks breaking Keyan's routine and potentially ruining the start to his day (and mine too—because if he is not happy then I am not happy). It's an example of how little things in our lives can be stretched into something big—potentially meltdown worthy. So having a mountain of T-shirts helps minimize the potential of a breakdown—on his part and mine.

When Keyan Is Sick

When Keyan is not well, all bets are off. If he wants ice cream for breakfast, then that is what he gets. If he wants to be alone, then we leave him alone. If he wants to sleep in my bed, then he sleeps in my bed. Caring for Keyan on a good day is draining, but when he is sick, it is beyond exhausting. Not only are we physically running around caring for him, but we are emotionally spent, too. There is a saying that "A mother is only as good as her weakest child."

Sadly, when Keyan doesn't feel well, he can't ever tell us what is wrong. We have to decode his behaviour to understand what might be going on. If he loses his appetite, often it's because of a sore throat which we can detect with bad breath. When his eyes are glossy it usually indicates a fever. When he wakes up more frequently at night or wants to stay home, that is another indication that something is off. We have become really good at the process of elimination. It is not an exact science—our goal is always to make him comfortable while his body heals itself.

An added challenge is that Keyan doesn't help his own cause. Often, when he has a sore or scab, he will pick at it, making the problem worse. Once he had a tiny sore close to his mouth but because it annoyed him he played with it; half of his face was red, scabbed, and inflamed. The scariest part was how hard it was to get the swelling under control.

Another time, the effects on him were so horrible that it felt as though our son was possessed and needed an exorcism. He ran around the house screaming his head off, banging the walls, and contorting his body in ways we'd never seen. I was afraid he would sprain, twist, or break his ankle—that is how violent his movements were. There was nothing we could say or do to make him better. Kunal took two days off of work because neither one of us could care for him alone. If we brought him to the hospital in his current condition we knew they would have to heavily sedate him, to the point of knocking him out. I could just see his hands strapped to the bed in order to keep him from running away or pulling out IV lines. One of the biggest fears Kunal and I share is having to bring Keyan to the hospital, where we envision them treating him like an animal.

To give you perspective, we can't even get a Band-aid on Keyan. When he cuts himself it is an enormous stress for us. He won't allow us to tend to his wounds like a normal child. Instead, to clean a cut, we have to put him in the shower. If the wound is on his feet, we have learned to immediately put clean socks on him after the shower. If it is elsewhere on his body we put him to bed, encouraging him to relax. We lay beside him to offer comfort and stay with him as long as it takes for the blood to clot. It is our way of helping him heal and it also saves us from cleaning blood from all over the house.

At the end of October 2020, the world is exhausted. The United States elections are next week, the coronavirus is still killing too many, and the things that plague our world are omnipresent: racism, global warming, extreme poverty, etc. Keyan is not well, and we don't know what it is. We can assume he has COVID-19, but he does not have a fever. Headaches and lack of taste are things we cannot confirm. He does have a skin infection that we have been treating and have under control. This time it's strange—he has started crying. Listening to Adele at the kitchen table, he sits there vocalizing sadness, as tears stream down his face. He does this for a week. I don't try to sway him to feel a different way. Instead, I conclude that it's cathartic for him to cry and to be able to release how he feels.

We Stop to Dance

There are days I wake up in a bad mood, with no specific reason as to why. On one particular occasion, I was getting mad at myself for being this way as I scurried around the house doing dishes, laundry, and preparing Keyan's breakfast. I started to question myself, What the hell is my problem? Why am I in such a bad mood when I slept so well? I didn't go to bed angry. I'm not sick. I thought moving around to get more things done would help me to feel accomplished, but it made me more aggravated.

Then I stopped everything I was doing and took a deep breath. I thought to myself, If I don't change my mood I will be miserable for the rest of the day. Breathe. What can I do to change my state of mind? Then it came to me. The answer was to move—sweat, run, get the blood in my body circulating. Although I didn't feel like working out because of my long to-do list, I needed to get out of this funk. I changed into my workout clothes and headed downstairs to my home gym. I scrolled Spotify and landed on one of my favourite artists—Macklemore. "You know I'm back, like I never left-Another sprint-another step." The words could not have been more perfect. While I was getting my shoes on, Keyan appeared from what we call his light room.

Before I continue with my morning, let me tell you about Keyan's room. In the basement, we have two storage rooms. One is quite large and houses a "Mama Bear" office, the furnace, the water heater, and Christmas decorations. The other is a quarter of the size, and we call it "Keyan's room." It has shelves on every wall and reminds me of a youth hostel. On the floor, we stack sleeping bags, blankets, and pillows to create a soft landing spot for him. This small space gives a sense of being cocooned. Keyan often goes there after school to unwind from his day. It is similar to the Snoezelen rooms they have in many special needs schools, which are created to calm people. One of its features is different coloured lighting—similar to what you find in a spa. We installed a string of LED lights in Keyan's room that would provide the same effect, changing colours from blue to green, yellow, and orange. There are different settings depending on one's mood. The room is a huge success, and if we are lucky enough—most people aren't—we are invited in for a little snuggle.

That morning, Keyan stood outside of his room with his eyes closed and his fingers in both ears. He was humming. Because he cannot speak to me, I like to connect with him through touch. I advanced slowly so that I didn't startle him and gently wrapped my arms around him for a hug. Next thing I knew, his arms were around me. There was a gentle swaying from side to side as though we were slow dancing—then I realised, hey, we are. Instead of being concerned about getting my workout done, I made the conscious decision to be all in—to be present in this very simple but magical moment. We continued to sway and I closed my eyes to block out all other senses. I felt his hands on my back, his head on my shoulder and the weight of his body. Although he stood at almost six feet tall and weighed 160 pounds, at this moment he was weightless. He felt like he did when he was an infant—safe and happy in my arms. I pushed the world away and thought only of this moment. I breathed one big inhalation and smelled his hair. My thought was that this man, this boy, this babe, will always be my baby. I wanted this moment to last forever. We continued swaying—even changing the rhythm at times. My mood was completely changed. I felt gratitude wash over me. I felt the connection between mother and son. I was close to tears, but before they fell he released me.

Thank you for the dance, my son.

PART II

The Middle—Feels Like a Fight

You Can Call Me Mom

When Keyan was diagnosed with autism, I had a painstaking decision to make: would I take on the role of being his mom, or would I become his therapist? You might think the choice would have been obvious, but having lived through it, I can tell you—you have no idea the hell I went through. When your child is newly diagnosed, you feel a desperation to do anything to provide them with all they need to succeed. While many experts push for "early intervention," there are incredibly long waitlists of over two years and exorbitant rates for private therapy which exceed one hundred dollars an hour. I felt constant pressure to study and best understand how to stimulate my child with the goal to take him out of his bubble and bring him into our world. When my precious little boy was only a year and a half old, I felt paralyzed. I couldn't even do a puzzle with him. The thought of being a therapist to him (a choice a lot of mama bears make) frightened me to death, and so I took the other route and decided to be his mom. I wanted more than anything for my children to feel safe with their parents—in our home—in our lives. I feared Keyan would hate me for pushing him out of his bubble. My logic told me that I could pay any number of therapists to help him, but only one person could ever be his mother.

As he grew older and other children on the spectrum seemed to progress nicely—I felt guilt. Did I make the right decision? Maybe I could have taken Keyan further in his development had I applied myself more, had I forced myself to work with him—work *on* him. I watched as other children played sports, learned to speak and read, and attended regular school. In fact, these children were on the spectrum and didn't know it—their parents only told them much later in life. Was it because of me that Keyan wasn't progressing as quickly?

As part of trying to find answers, I attended a three-day conference in Toronto in 2018. I listened to speakers from Canada, Belgium, and the United States all covering different topics related to autism. It opened my eyes to new research, validated things I already knew, and reminded me how hard it can all be. At one point I sat in the audience wiping away tears as they streamed down my face. It was informative but obviously very emotional.

However, most of the conference focused on higher functioning individuals, which left me feeling like an outcast in a group where I had thought I would fit in. Having left my family for three days, I needed to get something from this conference. I had to allow myself to feel the hurt, discomfort, and disappointment in a space that wasn't focusing on the kind of autism my son had. I thought, What can I take away from this event? It can't be a waste. I reminded myself that I was there to learn and take away with me every golden nugget. I gathered so much information that I ended every day exhausted, my brain feeling like it was going to explode.

And then I began to find the answers I was looking for. Speaker after speaker emphasized that people living with autism experience the world differently, and if we pay close attention we can see what they experience. Without exception, a person with an autism spectrum disorder lives in a constant state of anxiety with a number of sensory issues (which present differently for each person). I reflected on seeing the world that Keyan experiences and thought about how this relates to my own experiences. I don't have autism, but I have a severe anxiety disorder and an array of sensory issues. Flickering lights, escalators, blowing fans, heat—all of these things bother me. When I am uncomfortable in my own skin, I can potentially have a panic attack. I have learned to manage most daily occurrences, but when I am out of my element, like when I travel, things become more difficult. I understood how my son was much like me.

Another golden nugget I took away from the conference was that if we address the anxiety and sensory issues of people with autism rather than focusing on pushing them outside of their bubble, we are likely to have a better outcome. Although it took many years for me to release myself from the guilt of not having done more for Keyan, I knew that at every turn I had given him both the emotional safety of his mama and the required therapies from others. The conference validated for me that I had made the right decision in focusing on my role as a mom.

A Shift in Perspective

"No, autism is not a 'gift.'
For most, it is an endless fight
against schools, workplaces, and bullies.
But, under the right circumstances,
given the right adjustments,
it CAN be a superpower."

-Greta Thunberg

A big part of who I am and what I want my children to be are people who live in service to others. Even if their careers didn't define them as such, I envisioned them taking part in mission work, or working in soup kitchens to feed the hungry, or volunteering in after school programs to help underprivileged children. I firmly believe that an enriched life includes helping those who are less fortunate.

A diagnosis of autism didn't mean that Keyan couldn't do those things. Autism is a spectrum of people with all kinds of abilities and disabilities. We know individuals who are on the spectrum who go on to lead wonderful lives without too much help. Take, for example, the character Sheldon

Cooper on the popular sitcom The *Big Bang Theory*. Despite his quirks, he lives a full life doing what he loves, surrounded by people who support and accept him for who he is. Keyan, however, never acquired language, and it was also obvious that he had an intellectual disability as well. Taking those three things and marrying them—autism, lack of speech, and an intellectual disability—meant the end of my dreams for my son.

Like many others, I had a limited belief in what a person like Keyan could do. I saw individuals with significant special needs as non-contributors to society. We are so conditioned to think a certain way—that there is right or wrong, black or white, and positive or negative. But that is rarely the case. It is just like there is not one right way to raise a child with autism, and the textbooks or manuals that claim to know—I call bullshit. It is impossible to write about autism and get it right, because there are twenty-one different medical or psychiatric conditions that can exist alongside it. That means an individual will most times not only have autism, but also have several other issues to deal with. It is rare that an individual will only have a diagnosis of just autism. I am not saying it is impossible, but it is rare.

I found myself obsessed with what people thought of my son. How did they see him? I could feel the pity and judgement. The whispers. I could sense them. "Poor Audrey and Kunal—what they have to endure with Keyan—how do they do it?" Couples admitting to one another, "I could never do it. Bless them." I don't think I can exempt anyone I know from having those thoughts. Truth be told, if the tables were turned I would feel the same. A son that would never do so many things. The perpetual child—always needing his parents, depending on them, and never amounting to much in the eyes of society.

How could a person that needs constant care live a life of service? Impossible, one would think. We often work from these kinds of assumptions, but sometimes things are not as they appear. This realization hit me like a ton of bricks during an interview about emotional intelligence. The interviewer asked me what I wanted my legacy to be and I said it was for my children to be contributors to society. I talked about how my daughter, Manisha, is very intelligent and empathic and would do great things with her life. We spoke of Keyan, and I said how I had aspirations for him that would never manifest the way I had hoped. Then the lightbulb went on and I had an aha moment: the reason I was being interviewed at all was because of Keyan. It had to do with the advocacy work I was doing in honour of my son. In that moment it became clear that Keyan, despite not having the words or the capabilities himself, had a mother that was advocating not only for him but also for others just like him. I was Keyan's vessel. He was born the teacher and I was his student. I would pay close attention and go about doing the project assigned to me. Keyan would be a contributor to society because he would be the reason why both the Autism Awareness Run and S.Au.S. were born. He would be the reason why hundreds of families over the course of a decade would benefit from leisure programs and find a safe space to be themselves.

I like to use analogies or metaphors to make a point. Let's use Terry Fox and his Marathon of Hope: In 1981, Terry set out to raise awareness and money for cancer research by running across Canada. He managed to run across six provinces before he had to stop. For thirty years now, other Canadians have taken up where he left off by running in his honour for cancer research. The Marathon of Hope has raised over $750 million. Did Terry do all that? No. He was the catalyst, just like Keyan was the catalyst that started the Autism Awareness Run and saw the birth of S.Au.S., a charitable organization that would make a difference in our small corner of the world.

Over time I have come to see that what appears to be done by just one person is not so. It takes the love and support of others to help us achieve our goals. Terry Fox had the love and support of his family while he ran his marathon of hope, and after he succumbed to his cancer, they carried the torch for him. His family would ensure that his work would continue. So the questions we need to ask ourselves are, did Terry have a purpose, did he live in the service of others, and did he leave a legacy? If you answered yes, then I would agree with you. That is how I have come to see Keyan. Keyan being born with an autistic brain and being unable to speak didn't limit his power to impact the world. I would be his conduit to deliver the message that I valued the most and saw in my son: every human being has a right to live their best life, with love, dignity, and respect regardless of their abilities or disabilities. That is what I advocated for Keyan and how I became his voice. As mothers, we know what our children need, and because society hadn't yet figured out how to help and handle a boy like Keyan, I would show them how.

Do I Really Belong Here?

I was sitting in a room full of PhDs at McGill University for a conference focused on action research and its merits. Action research is an academic approach that identifies a problem and then creates concrete action plans that outline best practices. It's about taking action, doing research, and then using critical reflection to understand what works and what doesn't. All of the work I had done to build S.Au.S. in order to meet the needs of the autism community was action research. Walking the halls of the conference, I asked myself—how did I get here? I felt so out of place—as though someone had made a grave error in inviting me here. I quickly chased my negative thoughts away and decided to make the best of it—to take it all in.

The conference was set up so that there were several talks going on at once. The program provided the speaker's name and a brief description of their talk. In the first one I chose to attend, I was immediately captivated by the speaker, an energetic and passionate woman. I have to admit that I was more attracted to her passion about the topic than I was to the topic itself. Towards the end of her lecture I was mortified when she started asking every person in the room to introduce themselves. Some were introducing themselves in ways I didn't understand, as though they were speaking a foreign language. I could feel myself starting to sweat and I began to feel lightheaded. I wanted to shrink myself so no one would see me so that I could avoid having to speak. Why? Because the truth was that I felt inferior to everyone around me. It was almost like if I spoke that they would figure out that I was a fake, wasn't one of them, and maybe should not even be there.

My mind was whirling. What was I going to say? I completed a bachelor of arts in history more than twenty years ago. I mean, this was a room full of lifelong learners and real academics; some people even had two doctorate degrees. As soon as I opened my mouth, they would see that I was a fraud. My imposter syndrome kicked into high gear; all I wanted to do was to run out of the room because she was getting closer to me. I reminded myself that I hadn't been invited because of my formal education, but rather because of the work I had been doing for the autism community. According to my dear friend Judy, who invited me to partake, I was there to share my experiences as the president and founder of S.Au.S. I could do that. If Judy thought I was in the right place, regardless of the missing letters after my name, then I trusted her. My turn came and it took everything I had not to crawl under the desk. Who am I? That's a loaded question! Sometimes I feel like I don't even know myself. Where to start?

I start at my root chakra: "Hi, my name is Audrey Burt. I have a bachelor of arts in history." Immediately, I move to my heart chakra and open with, "I am a mom of two beautiful children, Manisha and Keyan." Without warning my throat chakra opens up and I find my voice. I explain that the driving force behind the work that I do for the autism community is my two children. I consider myself "a mama bear" who is grossly protective and is ready, willing, and able to do anything for her children. It all feels so surreal; I am now floating above myself. I can't even believe the words coming out of my mouth. They are so basic and don't seem to fit being at McGill University in a room full of highly educated individuals. Though my educational pedigree is simple, my words come out wrapped in an immense degree of passion and heart. My usual self would feel embarrassed by my vernacular; instead, the energy of the people in the room has served as fuel and I suddenly feel confident that I have something real to contribute to this conference.

The next part of my introduction is centred around Keyan's autism and my reasons for starting S.Au.S. I talk about how I had been desperate to create a safe space for my son and how I wanted him to have access to leisure programs he otherwise had been denied. My core belief is that all children should be granted the right to play in a setting conducive to their needs. My son was not given that, and so I was going to create that for him. I refused to watch my son and others like him be cast aside because they did not fit into society's perfect mould. I don't believe in disregarding anyone. I told the story of how the organization began.

Before I knew it, my introduction was done. All of the prejudgements of feeling not good enough melted away. I started to shift in my seat to sit a bit taller, shoulders back and head up. I no longer felt like the imposter—I belonged. All the PhDs seemed to understand better than me why I had been invited to join the conference. They saw a woman in the throes of living out action research in real time and wanted to support her while she was here, to equip her with information, to support her work.

There was a break between sessions and I met up with Judy and the other individuals she had invited to speak. Upon seeing an old colleague of mine, I instantly felt like a kid in high school hanging out in the lounge with friends to catch up on weekend shenanigans. I hadn't seen Martin in a few years, but he exuded positive energy and charisma. He is the type of person that always wants to make you feel welcomed and comfortable. He gave me a big hug. It was as though no time had passed since we last saw one another. I met Lynda and Laurie, and listened intently as they openly discussed how nervous they were to present. I was not alone in how I felt. I would have to wait until the afternoon block of the second day to present my topic. Feelings of anxiety built, like a pressure cooker wanting to release its steam. Martin was luckier as he got to present in the afternoon of the first day. When I attended Martin's presentation, memories of my days at Heritage Regional High School came flooding back. How I missed those days in the classroom. I missed everything about it, especially my colleagues and the students. That chapter of my life as a substitute teacher was amazing. I sometimes fantasize about going back, but then the reality of raising Keyan hits and I know that I no longer have the same energy that I did ten years ago.

The conference concluded and I came away with a renewed spark of enthusiasm for the future. All this time I was doing action research and didn't even know it. The conference affirmed that trusting my intuition and following my instincts had been the keys to my success as the head of S.Au.S. I knew what families raising children on the spectrum were missing and I was determined to provide it for them.

An Incredible Honour

Oftentimes I will bring myself to the brink of a breakdown when trying to accomplish something significant, whether I am training for a marathon, organizing a fundraising event, or simply taking care of Keyan. Whenever I reach my goals I don't know how to fully embrace the achievement. I don't allow myself to have access to the positive emotions I should be feeling. It's as though at a deeper level I don't believe I deserve the accolades.

I was called to the nation's capital to attend the Canada's Volunteer Awards, where I was to receive the highest honour ever bestowed on me. I was given the Volunteer Award for Community Leader for the province of Quebec. There were 266 applicants for this award category for which I took home top honour. When I first set out to demystify autism and help bring awareness to my community, I never thought beyond the immediate. My goal was always to raise awareness and make space in this world for my son and others like him. It is incredible to see where this work has taken me. I could never have imagined taking this stage.

What I really want to share with you is how it felt to be part of this ceremonious occasion—to be in a room with like-minded people from across the country—people who selflessly give of their time for others. I felt a great amount of pride in being Canadian. As I listened to everyone tell their story, I found myself in awe. My heart swelled with pride following each recipient's speech. How often do we get to take stock of our accomplishments? Not only to rewind, but to share with others. Even better, to be recognized by our government.

Before the official ceremony held on the evening of December 5, 2018, there was a two-day conference. On day one, all twenty-one recipients had five minutes to introduce themselves and talk about their volunteer work. So many amazing stories, so many hours given, so many people inspired, so many lives changed, and so many people helped. We started with eighty-year-old Harold, who had been volunteering since 1945 and was the Thérèse Casgrain Lifelong Achievement Award recipient; moved to Kaleb (who was sadly involved in the Humboldt Broncos accident), an emerging leader helping kids who have type 1 diabetes; to Oswald, who took home the Community Leader award (Prairies) and who shared his story of coming out of childhood abuse to help others. Stories of life, love, and loss that lead to lives dedicated to helping others. We also met the lovely organizers and reviewers who deemed our stories worthy of such honour. I immediately fell in love with Tina, a gorgeous Jamaican woman with a smile that lights up a room. She had nothing but praise for the work I do. To have someone clearly see the sacrifices that I made for the work I do felt like a gift in itself. Those who bear witness to my story as it unfolds seem tired of the things that I have to say, and maybe that's because they have heard them too often. To have had a captivated audience wanting to hear what I had to say was refreshing.

Day two was for round table discussions about the value of volunteering. We talked about the added value volunteering brings to a community. We agreed that volunteering is a catalyst for change within communities. It is essential to the wellbeing of any community we belong to whether geographical or cause-based. I have nicknamed myself the "nugget collector," because whatever I do and wherever I go there are always valuable takeaways—I call them golden nuggets. I take these with me to help bring S.Au.S. to the next level. Not everything valuable is found in a Google search. During these two days I collected so many nuggets. The most valuable one was a reminder that the work I do directly impacts the lives of others. I often lose sight of that because I am so hyper-focused on the organization and what needs to be done. I sacrifice my own experience for the good of S.Au.S.

I left the round table discussions feeling empowered, appreciated, and rejuvenated on a personal level. I had the opportunity to meet so many wonderful people and to share so many stories. For the first time in a long time, I felt a sense of belonging. I was overcome with gratitude.

Then it was time to receive our awards. The ceremony was steeped in formality. It felt regal. Everyone dressed for the occasion and buzzed with excitement. The handing out of the pins was done intimately amongst the recipients alone. A photo op included a Canadian Mountie at our side. The ceremony opened with a procession of the recipients walking a red carpet to their respective seats. The anticipation made me feel like a school child as we were lined up and shushed. The master of ceremonies was

Catherine Clark, the daughter of a former prime minister. She was incredibly articulate and masterful with her words. Davis Dewan sang the Canadian national anthem unlike any version I had heard before. Tears filled my eyes, but I held back. Next was an Algonquin prayer performed by First Nations cultural spiritual leader and Elder, Irene Compton. The welcoming remarks and awards were given by the Honourable Jean-Yves Duclos, Minister of Families, Children and Social Development.

We sat listening to each other's accomplishments read aloud, as per the program. I was tenth to be called to receive my award. I had two thoughts on loop: first, Don't trip on the stage, and second, Don't cry. As I stood on the stage I wanted to take it all in. I engaged with the guests by scanning the room to meet as many eyes and smiles as possible. I was in disbelief that this was really me standing on the stage in front of all of these amazing people and being honoured by my country. Incredible! It was all so surreal. I felt that I was not myself. They must have been talking about someone else. I mustered up the courage to allow myself to feel—but in a controlled manner, guarding myself from getting too emotional.

I stood by Minister Duclos as Catherine Clark read:

Driven by her commitment to creating a better life for her son and for children like him, Audrey Burt left her career as a substitute teacher in a local high school in order to dedicate herself to autism. Audrey built Soutien Autism(e) Support (S.Au.S.) from the ground up and has made an immeasurable impact on her community. S.Au.S. is a pioneer organization offering services where there previously were none. It operates in Candiac, Québec, a region that needs accessible services adapted to the needs of individuals on the autism spectrum. It was created by Audrey, but made possible by the community she brought together through the first Autism Awareness Run, followed by years of time and effort.

Audrey increased her impact on the community by creating a summer camp for adolescents on the autism spectrum. Knowing that children on the spectrum need a camp with programs and activities designed with them in mind, Audrey opened Camp Oasis in 2015, and has been welcoming children with Autism Spectrum Disorder (ASD) ever since. By holding many fundraising events and having regular volunteering positions in her programs, Audrey has provided many students from local high schools with the opportunity to contribute within their community.

Audrey's huge heart and philanthropy are now the driving force behind the plan to build a day centre for low functioning adults with ASD over the age of twenty-one who have no services available for them. It will welcome the maturing participants of S.Au.S. programs. Through all of her initiatives, Audrey effectively serves the participants of this growing community throughout their childhood, adolescence, and adulthood.

Through her years as a dedicated volunteer, Audrey has inspired many people and contributed endlessly to her community. Her story and her vision have touched many young minds.

Applause broke out in the room. I made eye contact with my husband and best friend, Chriss, who were in the audience. They registered my pride and I theirs. Minister Duclos turned to give me a gold framed certificate that reads Canada's Volunteer Award—Audrey Burt. Before I walked off stage, I scanned the audience one more time, taking it all in and registering how incredibly special this moment was. I was grateful for the acknowledgment of all the sacrifices I had made to meet the needs of the autism community.

Someone Hand Me a Lifeline—Please

At S.Au.S., we would often receive phone calls from families wanting to know about our programs. Many times, these conversations were about so much more. Take, for example, this call:

I answered the phone and a woman's voice was asking me about the services we offered. Before I could even say anything, she dove into the details of recent events concerning her son. Every time I tried to interject, she just continued. Her son's school had red-flagged him as having an autism spectrum disorder. (Understandably, it's as though a bomb has been dropped on her lap. She doesn't know what to do with this information. She talks as though once news like that is delivered, there should automatically be someone who shows up to guide, direct, and take care of her son. Sadly, it doesn't work that way. Our system is flawed in so many ways.)

I quickly realized she wasn't looking for programs for her seven-year old. Instead, she was looking for a lifeline—a person who would tell her that everything will be okay. The more she talked, the quicker her tears flowed. Her voice quivered as she explained that she knew her son was dealing with ADHD but she did not know that he also had autism. She made it sound as though autism was way worse. I beg to differ, but that is a whole other topic of conversation. I will say this—regardless of the diagnosis our child may have, it is because they struggle that we as parents struggle too.

My heart broke for this mom because I remembered how it was when Keyan received the diagnosis of autism. Speaking to this mom brought up all kinds of pushed down emotions. Although this was many years ago, the emotions attached to that time never vanish. Ask anyone who has had a heart wrenching miscarriage—we never forget those babies.

She explains to me that the school had dropped the bomb and she was left to pick up the pieces on her own. Yes, true. The school is there to educate students, not provide a plethora of services to support autism. It is tragic that there is no system set up to guide families and support them following an autism diagnosis. What that mama experienced is common. There is no fairy godmother put in our path to make things all better. I expressed that sentiment to her, saying that there is no one person that can help you. Instead, you have to be an information collector, obtaining knowledge from all different sources. Parents have to research, read, investigate, and advocate for their child. First, there is the infamous "Google search"; wherever that leads you explore it. By calling me, this mother wasn't merely in the process of collecting information, she was looking for a lifeline, hoping someone would tell her that her son wasn't autistic.

This is a prime example of how my job was often difficult.

Spending thirty minutes on the phone with a woman I didn't even know left me totally drained of all my energy. I am an emotional person to begin with, but a mama bear who is desperate and looking to me for answers had now been added to my day. I wanted so desperately to help, but I was helpless because I couldn't give her what she really wanted, which was to hear that everything will be okay. I had a full day planned and needed every ounce of my energy to get through it. That phone call totally derailed me. It's bittersweet at times, because I want to help but often it is at the expense of myself.

The most important thing I tell those who call me after their child is red-flagged for autism is that the child you have today will be the same child tomorrow. The only thing a diagnosis does is help you with the big picture. It enables you to get the proper tools to help you understand your child and hence help them live their best life.

This story is common and it belongs to all of us. Whenever someone is diagnosed with cancer, or a loved one is suddenly taken from us, or we suffer alongside a family member (for whatever reason), we need connection. We not only want answers but we need to connect with those who have a shared experience. We want to feel less alone, we need answers, and desperately want to change the situation, begging at times for things to be different.

The Bus Incident

There are days when it feels as though the universe is delivering a sucker punch to my gut. It almost always has to do with Keyan. It leaves me winded, dizzy, and disoriented. It is as though there is nothing I can do to keep me steady on my feet. That was how I felt when I learned about Keyan's bus rides to school.

On October 26, 2021, I received a message that Keyan had hit the bus driver. Upon learning about the incident, I called the bus driver. I called her for two reasons: first to apologize for my son's behaviour, and second to collect information by asking a series of questions.

In the back of my mind, I am always afraid that they will take away his transportation to and from school. I don't want to add "bus driver" to my already extensive resumé of the ways I assist Keyan. Already my days are consumed with laundry and food prep and acting as a personal care assistant, activity coordinator, and psychologist. I get drained, not from doing these things but from the amount of energy Keyan demands of me. I can't do more. If I have to drive him to and from school every day then I might as well keep him at home.

Line, the bus driver, accepted my apology. I wanted to know more about what had happened. Her answer to my first question was, "Your son punched me in my face." My mama bear heart wanted to scream to release myself of the emotions that rushed my system. Those words were more harmful than she realized. The irony is that my son Keyan is physically incapable of making a fist. So although I can't debate that he did indeed hit her, it could not have been with the attempted malice that she was conveying. I still had to give her grace because it is always scary when a man-child of 6 feet and 170 pounds comes for you. She didn't know Keyan outside of that bus so I couldn't alter the way she sees my kid. I could fully understand her shock. As Keyan's mom, though, I knew for a fact that he did not punch her, but he did still hit her.

I wanted to peel off the layers to understand what the trigger was—the why behind him hitting her. As I started my investigation, she kept saying that there was no reason and it had come out of nowhere. I tried to explain that Keyan is not aggressive by nature but that he can lash out if he is triggered. Keyan suffers from extreme anxiety, and if the adults taking care of him do not listen, things can go sideways quickly. When he feels unheard, he goes into fight or flight mode. His fight mode is a smack, a kick, or a pulling of hair. He can't speak, so the people in charge of him need to have the ability to recognize when he is starting to show signs of anxiety—anxiety that can quickly boil over. On this day, things got to be too much for him and he decided to let Line know.

The school bus drivers are not given proper training to work with special needs individuals. It is a tall order to drive a bus and know how to handle students who all have different needs. To make matters worse, the bus company and the school board don't assign students to their bus in a way that sets them up for success. Their goal is to pack them all in, like they do with regular schools, by mapping the routes geographically. This is a formula for disaster. Some kids are extremely vocal, and if too high pitched, the sound they make can penetrate others to the core of their being—it becomes akin to a form of aggression.

I relate this to a situation I had years ago while working at S.Au.S. I was in the midst of growing the team and the ladies liked to talk. I tried my best to curb their enthusiasm for the spoken word but I wasn't stern enough to get these grown women to keep the volume down. I was forced to take our three and a half-foot by nine-foot storage locker and turn it into my office (with a closed door) so I could concentrate. When I addressed this with my colleague, Nathalie, she said that the sound of other people talking never distracted her because she was used to working in big offices where there was constant chatter. I, on the other hand, needed a quiet environment to think. There were so many days that I couldn't execute my work properly because I was distracted by what everyone else was doing and saying. It is easy for me to become Keyan on the bus having to deal with the constant cacophony. I feel his anxiety and hence his suffering.

This is one of the hardest parts about raising a non-verbal child; he cannot tell us what is wrong. For the adults taking care of him, whenever there is an incident, it is vital to decode his reaction immediately. My line of questioning of the bus driver that day got nowhere. She merely kept repeating that there had been no reason for him to be triggered. Her words kept ringing, "Monster—

your son hit me and that makes him a monster." She felt reassured because the bus company told her that they would be installing plexiglass as a physical protection to keep her safe from the students. This is where the system is failing everyone—the driver shouldn't need plexiglass because the bus company and school board should be working together to match the students on the bus. When we focus on money, everyone loses—the students, the bus drivers, the teachers, and the parents.

There needs to be extra money spent on educating the bus drivers. They need to know more about their clientele. The school should also meet with the bus driver prior to the beginning of the school year to discuss each student— how each of them functions and their possible triggers. If the bus driver likes to play loud music but it can potentially trigger a student, then no music should be played. Keyan doesn't need conversation. He can't speak and when people talk to him he knows they expect something that he can't deliver. It makes him anxious. Besides saying hello, conversation with Keyan should be kept to a minimum. It doesn't matter how many times a bus driver says, "Good morning, Keyan," he will never be able to say it back. This is where it is essential to get to know the file of each student before driving them. Systems should be put into place to ensure a positive outcome for the students, rather than later having to deal with conversations with the bus driver and the school psychologist. Harnessing a child as a solution should be a last resort. For those who don't know how a harness works, it is a belting system that restricts mobility. This contraption makes the student unable to move and it is therefore very traumatizing for both the student and the parents. It makes parents feel that their child is being dehumanized. Regular school buses don't even have seat belts, but we have devices that feel like straight-jackets for our special needs children.

Not even a week after Keyan hit his bus driver I got an emergency call from the transport director, asking me to go get Keyan off the bus in the neighbouring town of La Prairie. He was having a complete breakdown. As I was getting my outdoor attire over my pajamas, I reflected and said, "If the bus sits idle, waiting for me to pluck Keyan off, it will worsen his behaviour." The man I was speaking to, I came to find out, was the same man who let the ball drop. He was supposed to process the bus driver's written report about the hitting incident so it could be delivered to the school. How ironic that the day I was summoned for an emergency was the same day we were to discuss the now ten reports compiled against my son, each representing a separate incident. I strongly believe that this current emergency was being used as a means to deflect from the fact that the director failed in a big way. There never should have been ten reports delivered to the school all at one time. Standard protocol calls for every single bus report to be processed within twenty-four hours. This provides an opportunity for everyone involved to work together as a team to figure out how to better support the student. When the protocol is ignored, there is a domino effect: the student isn't well, which negatively affects the other students on the bus, and then the teachers have to deal with the resulting behaviours in the classroom. And when the student comes home, they lash out at the family. Additionally, if the initial situation is not resolved, the student's behaviours of concern that occur on the bus may repeat or escalate because the student is not being heard. All of this was preventable had someone done their job!

My question to the director was, how can we help to

address problem behaviours or situations if they are not brought to light right away? He admitted that he had failed to process the complaints against Keyan immediately after they had come up, and the way I saw it, he had used Keyan's behaviour to cover up where he had fallen short. Pardon the pun, but imagine throwing a special needs person under the bus to save your own ass. I just can't understand how some people are willing to lay blame on a special needs individual rather than hold themselves accountable. It is situations like this that make it hard for me to trust the people who take care of my son.

Oftentimes it is not our child that makes this journey difficult but rather how others view him. I am painfully aware that some people see my son as less than or, even worse, not deserving of life. As a society, we haven't been properly educated on how best to treat people with special needs. There is a real lack of trying to understand those who are not like us and we need to find ways to bridge the gap. I often hear echoes of parents saying, "Not my child, therefore not my problem." The sentiment haunts me. A society shines brightest when its people take care of each other. Societies where the healthy take care of the sick, the rich take care of the poor, and the young take care of the old have a superior quality of life—for everyone. Here it feels as though everything is divided.

I had, in the end, spoken to the bus driver, the school vice-principal, the psychologist, and the school board. I had insisted that Keyan be given another transport. He had been utterly traumatized by the bus rides to school and this had been proven by the fact that he had so many reports against him—something we had never experienced before. I had to explain that all of this was affecting his overall well-being. He doesn't know how to let go of everything that has happened. He carries the stress with him day and night.

Keyan did end up getting assigned to a different bus, but sadly did not fully recover. It was Keyan alone who ultimately suffered the long-term consequences. His behaviour was altered, and so we had to have several meetings with the school. We had to change his medication and keep him home more than ever before. I hoped a joyous summer break would help him to forget and give him a fresh start in the fall.

Defending Him

I despise the false narrative that moms to special needs children are emotionally and irrationally charged. For me, I will admit that when Keyan was very little it was harder to cap my emotions. After all, I was navigating uncharted territory. There is no manual or *New York Times* bestseller on how to raise a child with a plethora of special/high needs. As Keyan gets older, it is imperative that I remain calm and focused for his protection. The more information I gather, the better equipped I am to defend him. I have become an expert in reading between the lines. I know words have power and I use and interpret them very carefully. This skill helps me piece together any scenario involving my son.

I am more than a mother, I am also an advocate. All moms to special needs kids have to be. We are our children's voices.

I am going to say something that is going to be extremely unpopular—not all moms are created equal. (I can hear the snapbacks now.) Some mothers check out as soon as their children show any signs of independence. Often this happens in adolescence, when the children get their driver's license, a part time job, and someone to love.

Maybe I am somewhat bitter because I don't have the luxury of letting go. I am in it for the long haul. Keyan will be in my care until I am no longer able to care for him.

The Keyan Chronicles (Facebook)

When I was a child, I spent a lot of time at my grandparents' house including lots of sleepovers. In early adulthood I even went to live with them. The first thing my grandfather, Al, would do every morning was to walk the long corridor—his slippers clacking against the floor—in order to pick up the newspaper that had landed at the front door. He would then go to the kitchen, stretch out the pages across the table (this took up the whole surface), and proceed to read it from start to finish. By the time I became an adult, most things had gone digital, so for my own daily morning read, social media was what I turned to. I was always more interested in people than money, religion, or politics, which is why I chose Facebook as my source. I absolutely love connecting with people that I haven't seen in a long time. I was always particularly curious about people that I went to high school with. Facebook helped feed that curiosity.

Social media has been an incredible tool for me to use. I believe that the birth of Facebook helped me both personally and professionally. It helped garner visibility for the Autism Awareness Run in its infancy, and later on it helped to disseminate important information about S.Au.S. On a personal level, it allowed me to share my life as mom to Keyan and that helped me to feel less alone. It is here that I learned the lesson that everything happens for a reason. Posting content on a regular basis helped me to gain confidence as a writer. People would comment on my posts or send me private messages, often complimenting me on my ability to articulate my thoughts. This later gave me the courage to build a website that would be home to A *Mama Bear* blog.

The truth is that Keyan is the star of my social media. He always gets the most likes and comments. He has his own segment that I call "The Keyan Chronicles". Whenever he does something new, funny, or educational (a lesson on autism) I post a video along with a description of what is happening. People love it! My motivation is always to give people a glimpse into our world to help demystify autism.

Facebook Post February 6, 2018
I have heard many people say that they strongly dislike social media because they think people are fake. They tend to believe that people only share the best of themselves: selfies/photos (with filtered faces), exotic vacation pics, and endless stories of their success (athletic endeavours, new jobs/promotions, bragging about how many goals their kid scored, etc.). Let's not forget the endless thank you for the great dinner last night, "I have the best friends," and "that was one hell of a party" (yup, the one you weren't invited to).

Then there are those who live with a negative mindset. They use social media mostly to creep others and to criticize others in an attempt to make themselves feel better about themselves. There are tons of creepers who never comment, or worse, they do and it's nothing but venom. There are people who talk about the fight they had with their spouse, post a meme with passive aggressive undertones, or post stories about strangers who did them wrong.

This is where I struggle with my life as a mother to an autistic boy; I feel strongly compelled to raise autism awareness (acceptance). I sometimes fear putting myself, my son, and my family out there. My life is so difficult that I don't need the criticism. Where is the line between sharing the right amount and sharing too much? I want people to know and see the good, the bad, and the ugly. When things are good they can share in our triumphs and when things are bad they can have empathy, extending a kind word.

For some reason I feel compelled to share this with you. Tonight, my son came home from school in a wonderful mood, happy and smiling. After supper I took him to his semi-private music therapy class (his favourite activity on the S.Au.S. calendar). Unbeknownst to me, the other parent showed up fifteen minutes late; this interrupted the lesson which didn't sit well with Keyan, sending him into a tailspin. I was called to pick him up. I was fuming because in the parent contract there is a "no-late policy" to avoid these types of situations.

While back in the car I decide to film Keyan to record how distraught he is. He is yelling and banging on the windows. He is rocking back and forth red faced and in tears. It looks scary to watch someone have a complete meltdown. We are both safe but emotionally spent.

Allow me the opportunity to describe what you see and feel from two different perspectives: Keyan's and mine

Keyan's perspective (if I could get into his head)

Damn those people for coming into class late; they should know better. Now I feel unsettled, disorganized in my brain, and incredibly anxious too. Something is off and I can feel the frustration bubble up inside of me. I have to let them know that I am not okay and the only way I know how is to escape to the bathroom, bang on the walls, and yell. Now I am the one disrupting the music class, but it's not my fault. They are the ones who threw the class off by showing up late.

What happens next? The teacher, fearful that Keyan might break the mirror in the bathroom and hurt himself, calls me. I tell her that I am on my way and will be there in five minutes (I am always close by since the class only lasts for forty-five minutes). I am pissed at the other parent who has had no regard for the other students. Although I had implemented a no-late policy when I was running the programs for S.Au.S., it had clearly been ignored and both Keyan and I were the ones to suffer the consequences.

My perspective
I feel his desperation and him wanting me to fix it. Both he and I know that I can't. There is nothing I can say because talking at this point will only add to his frustration. For his whole life, even as his mom, I haven't been able to talk him out of a tantrum—instead, I quietly hold space for him while chanting silent prayers and hoping that he calms down and finds peace soon.

My heart is racing and I am starting to sweat. While Keyan is rocking he touches my shoulder and I feel guilty for my inability to make it all better. The more he cries, "Mama, Mama, Mama," the more my heart breaks. I am teetering between total rage (at the other parent) and sadness for my son. I feel hot. The car ride home is longer than usual.

I have to remind myself to breathe. There is no way for me to soothe my son. My only comfort is knowing that soon we will be home and he can then seek comfort in things that calm him: a snack, his iPad, or a shower. Damn the teacher for not following the rules, and damn the parent for not taking everyone else into consideration. I am going to have to follow through with this tomorrow. This ruins my whole evening—the scenario replaying over and over in my mind.

Supportive comments on the Facebook post came flooding in and it uplifted me. The video did what I had wanted it to do; it educated people on what autism sometimes looks like. I was reminded that Keyan is valued for who he is. It is not easy for a non-verbal person to experience the world this way, but there is sympathy for how he does that.

What Help Has Looked Like

I know people have good hearts and want to help but don't know how. For all of you who have been there for me, my sincerest thank you. Let me give you a small list of what that help can look like:

- Show up for me and my family.
- Acknowledge my challenges.
- Ask how I am.
- Bring me a coffee (yes, Tim's, one cream and one sugar).
- Support my work.
- Don't be afraid to ask me questions about autism.
- Ask how my children are doing.
- Let me vent.
- Be patient with me.
- Allow my tears to flow.
- Forgive me when I have done something wrong.
- Acknowledge that I am only human.
- Let me know when I have done good with my kiddies.
- Spend time with me: dinner, coffee, the movies, etc.
- Make me a cocktail.
- Bring me food (a special thanks to Lisa).
- Ask me about running (my passion).

- Join me on a drive with Keyan.
- Take my children for ice cream.
- Respond to my Facebook status because sometimes your messages give me the strength to carry on.

I think this list applies to any mama bear who lives with a special needs child. We don't always want to be mamas— we want to be women in our own right, too.

Fight or Flight

I want to do an exercise with you. Close your eyes. Take a deep breath. We are going to go back in time. Visualize your child as a baby, or think of one you were babysitting. Remember how stressed you were trying to decode "the cry"? One cry meant the baby was hungry, another that the baby needed a diaper change, and yet another that they wanted to be held. Sometimes after covering all the bases they still cried. How did that make you feel? Anxious, frustrated, or hopeless?

The cries tend to change from infant to toddler; they begin to mean more. Think back to the terrible twos when a cry meant, "Just give me what I want or I will throw myself on the floor and embarrass the hell out of you." Thank goodness that that was just a phase, because eventually your young child developed language and could request their wants or needs. Now open your eyes.

This is another piece of our complicated autism puzzle—Keyan can't speak. I am pretty sure he has a plethora of words in his head but his brain will not let them out. I know this because when I talk to him, his eyes speak to me. I can see him processing what I am saying, albeit most of the time he wants to ignore what I am saying. Imagine being in a world where your voice goes unheard. No one listens because you can't say a thing. This leaves Keyan forced to use other means of communications: sounds, body language, pictures, gestures, pointing, and so on. This was all fine when he was little and his needs were basic. When Keyan wanted cereal, he would walk over to the food cupboard and point to the cereal box. As he got older, his needs became more complex, and it was harder for him to communicate and more difficult for us to understand. How can he say to us, "I am scared, I am overwhelmed, I have a sore stomach, I think I have allergies, I don't feel myself, it's too noisy in here, something stinks bad, I have an itch on my back, I'm bored, I want to go somewhere, thank you for all you do mama, I have the best big sister, Papa—thanks for playing with me, I think she's pretty, my socks are too tight, there's no more gum in the house, I can't find my iPad, I love you guys." Without words, how can he convey these thoughts to the world?

At times Keyan has had issues with impulsivity, meltdowns, and aggressive outbursts. I often remind him that I accept him for all that he is and all that he isn't. But, the one thing that is extremely difficult for me to accept is aggressive behaviour. The only thing that I want is for him to be a GOOD BOY.

From the core of my being I cannot stand confrontation, fighting, or violence in whatever state they present. I keep reminding myself that the reason a person with autism may demonstrate aggressive behaviours is not the same as for a person with a neurotypical brain. Keyan has no cause to flex his masculine muscle to prove that he is stronger than another human being. His aggression is purely based in the encoded DNA that has been handed down to all of us from our Neanderthal ancestors who regularly faced life or death situations, causing them to go into "fight or flight mode." They did this because they lived amongst ferocious carnivorous animals who threatened the survival of their species.

You don't have to have autism to know what "fight or flight" feels like in your body. This response can present itself in very stressful situations to anyone. A perfect example is turbulence on an airplane. For some people, it makes hearts race, palms sweat, and it invokes thoughts of the plane crashing—invading or intrusive thoughts. In other individuals it merely means that the plane has hit an air pocket, and they don't allow their thoughts to run wild. People with an anxiety disorder will feel at times that they are in a dangerous situation when in fact they are not—it is their mind playing tricks on them. The stress of a certain situation will kick serotonin levels into overdrive, signalling to the brain to enter into either "fight" mode (defend oneself against some kind of danger) or "flight" mode (run away).

Lately, Keyan appears to be struggling with this "fight or flight " response. His neurodivergent brain paired with raging teenage hormones and the fact that he can't speak makes it difficult for us to decode what he is trying to tell us. Talking about Keyan's aggressive meltdowns is hard for me, because it makes me feel as though I am dehumanizing my own son. I want everyone to see what I see a boy with a kind soul who struggles to be understood. I always say that if he were "normal" he would be the kind and sensitive type. I know Keyan has a beautiful soul. Like his big sister, I picture people saying things about him that would make me swell with pride.

Keyan works with an internal compass that has two poles—up or down. This means that every waking moment is governed by whether something feels good or not. When it doesn't feel good, he wants out—he wants to quickly make those feelings stop. One situation in which he exhibits this is at the end of the school year, when students tend to get restless. The excess in movement, noise, and elevated anxiety in the classroom tend to stress him out—in essence, he no longer feels good. There is an expectation for him to stay in class when all he probably wants is to be at home and in the pool. Kunal and I work closely with Keyan's teachers and the staff to find solutions to help him get through the day the best he can. We want the best for him, but it makes our daily lives extremely challenging when we are interrupted by phone calls to come pick him up from school, mid-day. We want to avoid a total breakdown that sends him spiralling into crisis mode. We want him to know that we are listening to him when he says he cannot handle it anymore. It is our job to pay attention to his non-verbal cues and manage ourselves accordingly. Otherwise, we risk him going into "fight or flight" mode.

When Keyan decides to fight because he is not being heard, respected, or understood, it's not pretty. It is scary to see a six foot, 170 pound human with glazed eyes lunging to grab at you. When he gets into a defensive state, he will grab at your arms, kick, bite, and sometimes pull hair. It's admittedly terrifying if you don't know him. It's made even worse if you don't know how to de-escalate things. If ever you are near someone in crisis mode, the best thing to do is back away, use few words, and make sure that everyone can maintain a safe distance. Words cannot calm Keyan down at this point. He has to self-regulate by riding out his emotions. At school, there are special rooms used for calming down students. These rooms help block out all outside sensory input (sight, sound, smell, etc.) and they keep all students, teachers, and staff safe when there is a crisis. What do I do at home? I walk away to give him the space he needs to calm down on his own. I never ever touch Keyan when he is in fight mode. If he comes towards me I walk away. I wait for him to self-regulate. When he gets back to baseline we move swiftly forward. We focus on making him feel safe and loved.

Responding to Keyan in Crisis

There are things to take into consideration when Keyan is in crisis. These guidelines can also be used when dealing with other individuals on the autism spectrum.

- It's important not to take things personally. Whatever they say, or whatever actions they take, such as trying to kick, grab, or bite—it is merely in self-defence.

- Though Keyan may kick, grab, or bite in self-defence, it's never his intention to attack or hurt people out of nowhere. A meltdown means that something has triggered him. Oftentimes, it means that the adults caring for him are not listening to his non-verbal cues. It can be tricky, since sometimes he lashes out when he is not feeling well and he can't tell us in what way he is not feeling well. He will never randomly attack someone. Never will he have pre-planned aggression where he picks up an object with the goal of hurting another human being.

- Sometimes, individuals with autism may get into a loop; they repeat the same things over and over.

It may seem aggressive if taken personally. They are really trying to self-regulate—so if someone tries to stop them, it escalates the situation.

- I have to allow him time to self-regulate. Usually, nothing I say or do helps. He needs time and space to process the situation. Talking at him doesn't help and it usually makes the situation worse.

- Intense eye contact is also troublesome—because he physically, mentally, and emotionally cannot deal with it. He knows there is some kind of expectation that he can't deliver on, so my advice is to divert your gaze.

- Language—use clear, short, and concise sentences. No need for details. Keep it simple. Keyan only has the capability to pick out key words.

- Tone and volume—a calm and soothing voice is always better for the individual that you are dealing with. Think of how you would talk to someone who is suicidal—you wouldn't yell at them you would use a calm voice to signal to them that they are safe.

- When Keyan has a meltdown he knows how to self-regulate. He simply needs patience and time. There is no reason to touch another human being. There are ways to diffuse a situation without ever touching someone.

- The fact that Keyan can't speak terrifies me. I can picture a scenario where a police officer is expecting him to respond to questions—only to be met with what would seem like non-compliance. I visualize a scene where the officer is becoming increasingly frustrated because my son is unable to answer any questions.

State of Repair

The source of our stress doesn't only manifest as a direct result of Keyan's behaviour towards people, but also because of the impact he has on objects. He wets the bed so we have to wash the sheets, he breaks the door so we have to fix it, he taps on the TV screen repeatedly so we have to replace it, he cracks a dish against the sink so we have to throw it out, he drops BBQ sauce on his shirt so we have to buy him another one (yes, I sometimes forget the stain remover), and the list goes on and on. There are times when he wrecks things and it's no big deal—at other times it overwhelms us.

At one point, he started a new habit of placing his iPad in the washing machine before heading into the hot tub. We call the hot tub the spa or to Keyan we refer to it as "the bubbles." He usually changes into his swimsuit in the laundry room. Without a place to put his iPad, he thought the washing machine would be good for safekeeping.

Well, wouldn't you know it—one day I turned on the washer without looking inside first. You can imagine my shock when I went to put the washed clothes into the dryer. The iPad was shattered into a million little pieces. Thankfully, it was in an OtterBox—one of those military grade cases—and this saved me the massive headache of cleaning out shards of glass from the machine and spending hundreds of dollars on a new one. However, we had no choice but to replace the iPad because it is a big part of Keyan's world. We had to rush out that very same day to get him a new one. It is one of the only things that gives Keyan something to entertain himself with. We need space from him at times.

Unlike other teenagers who want money to go to a restaurant, the movies, or shopping, we spend money repairing items that Keyan has broken. I can't begin to tell you how many iPads and headphones we have purchased over the years.

A Perfect Day

On September 22, 2018, we woke up at our usual time of 6:30 a.m. The weather felt more like typical fall temperatures, so Kunal brought me my coffee in bed. I looked at the headlines of the day on Facebook. Minutes later, Keyan joined us for a cuddle. I played *Frosty the Snowman* on his iPad because it signalled to Keyan's brain that I wanted us to stay in bed a little while longer. Once the twenty-five-minute video was finished, my son sprang out of bed to start his day.

Kunal was off to play golf for his buddy's birthday. He left soon after we had made our way into the kitchen. I had been so stressed during the past little while that in order to calm my nerves, I started organizing. Organizing my space is how I ward off stress. I had had new shelving installed in the laundry room and now I set out to finish the project by putting stuff back. After that was done I started to clean inside both stoves, empty the dishwasher, fold six loads of laundry, boil eggs, vacuum, and clean out the kitchen junk drawer. An unexpected full night's sleep gave me the energy to tackle these chores.

Now it's just Keyan and I. He started to indicate that he was getting bored. He had already taken a shower and sat in the spa. It was time to leave the house. I jumped in the shower for a quick wash. He granted me the time required to get dressed and blow dry my hair. With words I directed him to get dressed and he complied. As I scurried to gather my things I told him to brush his teeth. So awesome that he knows how—and even though he is not thorough, I am proud.

Without an agenda we set out on our merry way. Keyan was thrilled to be in his happy place—a moving vehicle. We made our way to the hardware store. We headed in. I asked him to push the cart for me to distract him from banging on all the signs and boxes that he saw. We wheeled through the aisles, and a miracle was bestowed on me—not only did I get the supplies I needed, but Keyan stood at the cash register without taking the candy or even asking for it. In fact, it's better than that—I asked him to put my wallet back in my purse for me and he did. He proceeded to close the zipper, too.

We wheeled the cart outside and he spotted the return area. Despite our purchases still being in the cart, he needed to put the cart back. He needed to do it immediately. I grabbed the items, and he shoved the cart into position against the others. He felt accomplished and so did I. Victory all around. And it gets better—I handed him my purse and he took care of it so that I could carry the purchased items safely to the car. Sounds like nothing, right? You probably go into the stores all the time without any issues. For us it's a big deal and we did it! Next, mama bear had to get herself a coffee. No biggie, we love the drive-through window. I took the usual medium coffee. I like to multi-task, so I placed my usual Saturday morning call to Dawn (one of my best friends in the whole world). She is such a ray of sunshine. She is the one person who knows how to keep me grounded, and she is a great listener who always makes me laugh with her wit. Keyan is used to hearing Auntie Dawn's voice as we drive. She is so sweet because she always makes sure to acknowledge his presence even though he can't respond. She said, "Bonjour, Keyan," and he waved.

I decided since Keyan was in a good mood that we'd run a few more errands. Off to the Corne d'abondance (equivalent to the Salvation Army) to drop off the clothes my children had outgrown. A quick stop at the S.Au.S. office to drop off the paperwork that I had been working on at home. Since Keyan was enjoying his time swivelling in my chair, I was able to follow up on outstanding items on my to-do list. With an upcoming gala event on the calendar, it was go time, and I couldn't waste a valuable minute. I am grateful that Keyan was cooperative, which allowed me to get a few things done.

One more errand. We headed to the farmers market. I couldn't keep food for long with a growing teenage son who ate anything he found. I replenished our fruit supply. What a glorious morning; I couldn't even believe it. Afterwards, we headed home because it was time for Keyan to eat again. I made him a plate full of fresh cut veggies, cheese, and rice crackers. He asked for something sweet and so I gave him cookies. He was still not satisfied so I dished out his favourite vanilla ice cream even though it was only 11 a.m. He deserved it!

Keyan was occupying himself nicely, so I finished folding the laundry, putting the clothes away, cleaning the stoves, and washing the floors. Now I thought I had done enough.

Keyan deserved a bike ride, so off we went. He was elated. He was simply so happy to experience the sound of the gentle fall breeze rushing past his ears. A day with both of us in sync. I was able to be productive while meeting Keyan's needs—sweet harmony. I trusted that after our action-packed day we would sleep soundly that night and I secretly hoped that it would be uninterrupted, too. A girl can dream.

A Cuddle Session with Keyan

The most wonderful things in life are the simplest. A smile, a laugh, a glass of wine, or a good meal. When we think of those we love, what we value most about them are the small things. It's not how much money they have, their postal code, or the awards they've earned, but rather how they make us feel. Keyan makes us feel all kinds of things. He is demanding of our time and energy, but having him as a son is magical. He forces us to see things that others take for granted. Now a young adult, my son still comes into our bed for cuddles and I get to hold him close and smell his hair. That might sound weird to you, but keep in mind that Keyan is like a four year old boy who seeks the comfort of his parents whenever he can. Think about the importance of touch—we all need it. Think of babies in orphanages who fail to thrive because of a lack of touch. Research has found that skin on skin contact for a newborn baby is essential to their wellbeing. Cuddling with my son is our non-verbal way of saying, "I love you son, you are safe, and we are here for you."

What does it feel like?

The warmth
His breath
His movements
Melting into my body
Pulling me towards him in a bear hug
The wanting to stay longer
His wanting to get out
His ripping off the blankets
Us bribing him not to leave
The moments when the three of us fall back to sleep
Breakfast in bed
All of us on our electronics
All so strange but all familiar to us
Feelings we never want to end
We envision this forever
So happy I bought a king sized bed
Three adults cuddled in safety and love

Forever Mine

My son cannot write his name, but he does recognize it when I call him. He cannot get himself a snack, make his own lunch, or cut up his favourite cucumbers—but he enjoys sitting in the kitchen while I prepare his food. He cannot wash his hair, thoroughly brush his teeth, or shave himself—but I am fortunate that he cooperates with me to do those things.

My son is severely autistic, which means that he will never be autonomous. He will never drive a car, live alone, or marry. Severely autistic means that Keyan is all mine. I will never be jealous because another girl has stolen his heart. I will be his first, last, and biggest love. He will only ever have eyes for his mama bear—those eyes that pierce my soul with intense love. Severely autistic means that we will always have a dependent, someone who needs us in every way, every single day of his life. The reality is that we will forever be caregivers, not simply parents guiding our children through life, but being there physically, financially, and emotionally as caregivers to our son.

The job of taking care of Keyan on a daily basis is a huge

undertaking. I always have to be on. There are days that I wonder if he is happy. When I think for one minute that he might not be, I become extremely sad. I have to chase those thoughts away or I risk succumbing to depression. I have to remind myself that Keyan's life is not as complicated as ours because he has no responsibilities or worries outside of the immediate. He doesn't worry about his future, because that concept in itself is too abstract for him. We are the ones that worry about his future and that is why I have to force myself to live in the moment. We have figured out what makes him happy and, lucky for us, it is all wrapped up in simple pleasures: swimming in the pool, going into the spa, swinging on his swing, enjoying a bowl of ice cream, bike riding with papa, or going for a drive with mama.

Camp Oasis

Keyan loves the week between the end of school and the start of the S.Au.S. summer camp that he goes to because, similarly to us, he feels as though he has control over his days: pool, spa, iPad, swing, bike, car ride, repeat. He can tell by the absence of his school bag in the morning that the day ahead is his. In order to help with the transition to camp, I got him a new backpack—a bright orange Camp Oasis bag to help signal to his brain that today is a camp day. I think thus far it has helped him tremendously to process things—he knows when he sees either his regular school bag or his new camp backpack that oops, "I guess I am not staying home today."

In 2016, I started the S.Au.S. summer camp for teens who are on the severe end of the autism spectrum. My thought process was that parents can make the choice to pay a babysitter to follow their child around the house all day to ensure their safety, or they can send them to our camp, which is designed to have teens doing activities that they enjoy alongside their peers in a safe and nurturing environment. When I think of Keyan home with a babysitter, I know he rules the roost. It is difficult enough for him to understand that not everything is about him, so I need him to be in a structured environment. Between organizing and monitoring the camp and ensuring that Keyan transitioned well into it, my summer had been very busy. The latter was out of my control. I did my best to prepare both Keyan and the camp team, but ultimately, he got to decide how things played out. I am proud to say that the usual transition to camp, which can take days or even weeks, this time took only two days. I think his level of comprehension had increased and he had matured somewhat.

Before this year, I had taken the summers off from S.Au.S. to recharge my batteries and spend time with Manisha while Keyan was at camp. This was the first summer that she worked full time, so she was no longer at home in the daytime. Also, with the amount of work we had at the S.Au.S. office and our plans for the future, I had to be present to push the agenda forward. My days were dotted with the time to recharge, rather than the entire weeks that I was used to for giving myself a rest. I welcomed the challenge. I felt that the ongoing work had kept me engaged, motivated, driven, and looking forward to the things coming down the pipe. With the promise that we had made to build a day center, which would provide much-needed services for the adult population who are on the severe end of the autism spectrum, we had our work cut out for us.

My heart is filled with pride when I think of my S.Au.S. team. A small office staff of only three women, we managed to do big things. Throughout the course of a year we organized a run in the spring, camp in the summer, and a gala event in the fall. These events welcomed hundreds of people and looked like they were put on by a staff of twelve. On top of that, we took care of the day-to-day operations and the leisure programs. Camp Oasis is the crown jewel of our programming. It is the only summer camp on the South Shore of Montreal that focuses only on teens with autism. It is my firm belief that clumping special needs individuals together is not in their best interest. Oftentimes, autistics and those with other types of intellectual disabilities don't mesh well together. I think it has something to do with the rigidity of the autistic brain. Therefore, we designed a camp specifically with the autistic camper in mind.

I can't say enough about the monitors at the camp. It takes quality staff to provide a quality service. Year after year, S.Au.S. is lucky enough to have many of the monitors come back, with minimal turnover. What that does is offer the campers a sense of comfort and stability. Camp stimulates Keyan in a bunch of different ways. First, he is surrounded by more people than he is used to. For example, at school there are only four students per class. At camp, there are on average fifteen campers and seven monitors for a total of twenty-two people per day, working alongside one another. He engages in a plethora of activities from art, to dance, music, walks, and sports. I get most excited when he successfully participates in the outings. His two favourites are iSaute (the trampoline center) and the local beach. The monitors at Camp Oasis do a phenomenal job of ensuring that every camper feels safe and has fun. It is an incredible feeling as a parent to know that your child is in a space where they are nurtured, respected, understood, valued, and loved.

A Bad Day Redeemed

This was one of those days that just started off on the wrong foot. From the minute Keyan woke up, it was one challenge after another. Totally off routine—he was all over the place: upstairs, down, loud, cranky, and defiant. It was one of those mornings that had me holding my breath, which is what I do when Keyan is stressing me out. I say little prayers—hoping that both he and I will survive the day.

Recently, I have come to the conclusion that we focus so much on Keyan's autism that we overlook the whole picture. This includes, struggling with impulsivity, dealing with an extreme anxiety disorder, and possibly going through puberty part II. I refuse to label my kid "the bad one," so I work hard to understand him. After all, I am his advocate and translator for the world.

After a delicate dance, I managed to get him off to camp. Phew—I could breathe, right? I wasn't off the hook yet. I readied myself to enjoy a lovely day with my sister, which included pedicures, lunch, and a quick visit to a cousin's house. But then the texts started to roll in. I felt rude picking up my phone, but I could see that the texts were from one of the camp monitors. I have to tell you, I don't have the energy to recount the whole story, but in a nutshell Keyan had a total breakdown where he bit a fellow camper and a monitor. The good part is that by the time she contacted me, Keyan was calm. I instructed her to bring him home and told her that I would be there as soon as possible.

I decided to stop in at the camp on my way home so that I could piece together the whole story of what had really happened. When I get a call or any kind of message about my son, I remain very calm so that I can use my energy to process. In this situation, I acted as Keyan's mom, the monitor's support, and the person responsible for the whole camp. My job was to make everyone feel heard, validated, and safe. I told the girls to write up a report on Keyan—because that is camp procedure.

I made my way upstairs to apologize to Keyan's fellow camper. The first thing I did when I saw him was to ask what happened. "Did Keyan give you a boo-boo?" He said, "Yes." I reached out to hug the boy and he immediately took me into his arms in a tight bear hug. I reciprocated by holding him just as tightly; it seemed to last a good thirty seconds. Within that brief period I was overwhelmed and started to cry. I whispered in his ear, "I am so sorry." Without words, I felt his forgiveness and he confirmed it when I let go and asked him, "Are you and Keyan still friends?" He responded, "Yes." My heart melted, because I have always loved this boy. At this moment I knew exactly why.

I walked away with mixed emotions—sad for Keyan's actions and touched by his fellow camper's grace. I thought to myself, These kids are incredible! I headed downstairs to talk to the head of the camp and the monitor that Keyan had taken a chunk out of (in case you are wondering, Keyan bit her finger). The victim of Keyan's rage was my niece. A big part of me was so embarrassed that he would do this to *her*, of all people. As she started to retell the events, I lost it. Instead of crying my face off, I simply got up to go to the bathroom to regroup. I came back when I was ready to listen. She continued to tell me the story. I listened and I was so proud because she had done exactly what she should have done in such a situation. At that moment I realized how much she had learned in the last two years of working at Camp Oasis. She is calm, compassionate, and has what it takes to work with people with special needs. We wrapped up the conversation and I again apologized for Keyan. I left the camp broken about my son, but beaming with pride over the team that I had assembled. Aggressive outbursts are the hardest thing for me when dealing with autism. They leave me embarrassed, exhausted, hopeless, and ashamed. It's okay that Keyan has autism but why, why, *why* the outbursts? Those are my dark times—when I feel truly hopeless about it all.

I came home totally deflated and left all on my own to deal with Keyan. As soon as he saw me walk in the door, he needed me to tend to him. It came in the form of a car ride first, followed by the endless buffet required to soothe him. I was exhausted and part of me was mad at him for ruining yet another lovely day that I had been having. Mad because I always have to be on for Keyan. He didn't understand that he had hurt me, that I was exhausted, and that I needed to be left alone. Mama, mama, mama—the only word he could say, and he had it on repeat until I gave him what he needed.

All I wanted to do was to lay down and cry. Cry away all my stress, frustration, and all the tears that my body could produce. Did I? Absolutely not!! Soon, Manisha would be home and I didn't want her to see me like that. After a day at work, she deserved to come back to a happy home. So the tears didn't come.

Kunal made his usual check-in call. When he asked how I was, I couldn't hide my feelings. I gave him an executive summary of what had transpired. He felt the same frustration that I had over our son's recent behaviour. I felt so lonely; in all of this, who was there to support me? It may make me sound petty or somewhat selfish, but it's because I was suffering. I told my husband that I needed his support. I am the one who has to deal directly with these issues, and yet I have had to find ways to comfort myself through it all. At that moment, he was incapable of offering the support I needed, and that was okay—he was simply making a check-in call and didn't expect to hear what I had to tell him. I wanted so desperately to have a shoulder, for him to allow me to cry and give me that, "Everything will be ok speech." But it wasn't there.

I don't know how else to describe my emotions from that day's events. I don't want to seem needy or weak, but that day I was. It was a bad day and all I wanted was to curl up in a ball and feel sorry for myself. There were often days like this, when I felt defeated and alone. What should I do? I picked myself up and soldiered on.

And I always try to find the silver lining in every situation—because *that* is what keeps me going.

I would be lying if I said that not one person reached out to me that day. The other monitor involved in this incident wrote me one of the most touching messages that I have ever received. This message is what finally got me to let out my tears:

Hi Audrey. I just wanted you to know that we are all okay and what happened today is water under the bridge. It is the reality of autism, and it is our job to take these things as they come. I hope you know that we do not think any less of Keyan, no matter the good days or the bad. He is a special boy with the most pure heart, and spending time with him is an absolute joy. We reminded Keyan's buddy that Keyan always loves him. And we always love Keyan too. Hope you guys have a great night. You're doing an amazing job, mama. Thanks for everything you do.

I replied:

This message means more to me than you will ever know. Please accept my deepest gratitude for taking the time to reach out. I appreciate you. – xox

Virginia Beach

The success of our annual, summer, family vacation to Virginia Beach is always contingent on one thing and one thing only: Keyan's mood. When he is good, we're good, and if he's not, then we're not. We spend a significant amount of our time and energy hustling to change his mood. It's a hell of a lot of work. I often wonder why I am so tired at the end of the vacation but the answer is obvious.

We rent a four bedroom, three-bathroom house for seven people on Chesapeake Bay. The other six members of our extended family spend the days with us in the house, but sleep in a campground five minutes down the road. It sounds crazy, but it works! Throughout the day from 8 a.m. to 10 p.m. we are thirteen to fifteen people all together, depending on whether my in-laws come or not. We have been doing this for twelve years now.

The sad part for me is that Kunal and I cannot sit on the beach at the same time, because Keyan needs constant supervision in the house. His limited capabilities mean that, aside from taking a clean apple out of the fridge, he cannot cut, pour, or mix his own food. In essence, his papa and I are short order cooks; we have to feed him every time he is hungry when we are supposed to be on vacation. He is a bottomless pit. When he is home, we spend our days in and out of the kitchen. Going on vacation does not stop Keyan's hunger pangs. In fact, when he is anxious or in transition, he finds comfort in food. He loves water and takes as many showers as he does snack breaks within the day. The kicker here is that he needs us to dry him off, or he simply puts on his clothes when his skin is still wet. Sometimes I just don't have the energy to keep up with him so I let him dry and dress himself, even if he is still wet.

Out of all the years that we have gone to Virginia, this was the year that Keyan decided to spend the least amount of time in the ocean. It's unfortunate, because he used to spend one to two hours in the water at a time. This year he decided that thirty minutes at once was enough. It felt as though as soon as he got in the water that he was already running out. His exiting the water meant that one of us had to jump up off of our beach chair and run after him to dry him off before he went into the house. His new thing was walking out of the house on his own to show us that he wanted to go for a car ride, which is one of his favourite activities. Yup, he is like a little dictator! Sometimes other family members yelled to me, "Audrey, did you know that Keyan is outside?" Damn. Once he was out of the house, we couldn't get him back in without first taking him for a drive, or we risked a meltdown of epic proportions.

THE DAY LOOKS LIKE
    Food
    Shower
    Food
    Ocean

Shower
Drive
Food
Shower
Food
Ocean
Drive Food
Food
Ocean
Shower

Are you exhausted reading this? Well imagine being part of the tag team that is forced to participate in this activity all day long—every day. We don't have a choice, so we do it. A few times we have asked Manisha to help out if she is sitting inside glued to her phone. This gives us just enough time to breathe, and then, before you know it, we are "ON" again.

So, why do it? Why go on this family vacation if it's so hard? The answer is that it is a long-standing tradition that means everything to the Saha family. We go because we are creating family memories with our children. Manisha gets to spend time with her cousins, and it's the one time of year that Keyan gets to jump in the ocean's waves. The adults spend time having intimate conversations—the kind where we share of ourselves: our hopes, fears, and goals for the future. The ocean facilitates things—it tends to open up pathways to this type of dialogue. I think it's magical.

I love having one-on-one time with each of my nieces and my nephew. We usually go kayaking or paddle boarding, or we take a walk, sit on the beach, or go out for ice cream. This year we bonded over the collective courage required to go into the "haunted house" on the boardwalk—it made us scream, laugh, and almost cry. I love the talks over morning coffee or in the early evening with a glass of wine in hand as the sun is setting. We sit on the beach to scan the ocean for dolphins, and when one of us spots them, hands start waving in the air with shouts of, "The dolphins are there! Look, look! The dolphins are there." Two lucky people get to paddle out to see the dolphins up close. This year I shared the experience with my older sister-in-law. We spent one and a half hours surrounded by dolphins. Pure magic!

This is also the one time of year that Manisha feels heard. She interacts with her cousins in ways that she can't with her brother. They spend hours in the water, floating on inflatable cushions and telling stories. Their laughter reaches the shore and it makes us smile. We wonder how much little people have to talk about. Manisha does most of the talking, and I am left to wonder if all of the conversations that she wished she could have with her brother are being expressed now. Another one of their favourite activities is collecting tiny crabs in sand pails. It becomes a competitive game of who can collect the most crabs. It is so beautiful to watch the cousins interact. The age gap has no consequence, and no one is cast aside. When Keyan goes in the water, the kids splash and play around him. He loves it!

When we come home, people ask me if I feel rested. I usually give a little giggle and respond, "It was a family vacation." It's the same amount of daily work, simply in a different location. Yet the time with our extended family is priceless; it solidifies our bonds and creates a lifetime of new memories. Although it's a lot of work for Kunal and I, we wouldn't have it any other way!

Letting Go of Assumptions

Being an empath and raising a special needs child is tough stuff. Both my son and I have sensory issues—Keyan because of his autism, and me because I am an empath. Ironically, what we want to feel or avoid are very different. Keyan feels the need to slam doors, bang on tables, and hit the walls. He loves to play with his vocal range and can hit a high note like Mariah Carey in "Dreamlover." It makes me cringe. All of the sounds and noises that Keyan makes is taxing on my nervous system. It's a constant barrage of overstimulating sensory input. This also includes his basement swing where he loves to swing, but also punch and kick the ceiling, sending vibrations up through the kitchen floor. Often, when the banging and vocals get too loud, I yell at him to stop. When I am at the end of my rope I'll yell, "Keyan, shut up." It's not nice, but in a strange way it makes me feel better; it's a physical release of my building frustration. When I look back, there are times when I don't know how I made it through the days of severe lack of sleep and sensory overload. Those times had me wishing that I could pack up and run away—if only to preserve my own sanity.

During the first summer of the pandemic we rented a cottage for just the four of us. On the fourth night in the rented cottage we had an extremely hard night with Keyan. During the day he had been antsy and had wanted to go in the car. I guess he was trying to tell us that although it had been nice up until now, he was declaring this vacation over. We can't always give into him. He got his revenge on us that night. He woke up at two different times, around 2 a.m. and 4 a.m. I had had a hard time falling asleep. I had just fallen asleep when Keyan woke me up for the first time. Kunal sprang out of bed to tend to Keyan. Now that he had woken up, I told myself that we were good for the night. I hoped that I would fall quickly back to sleep and I did. I didn't expect him to wake up for a second time because he normally wakes up only once. When he woke me for the second time it was as though I was experiencing sleep paralysis. I couldn't move. Then it was an early wake up at 6 a.m.—way too early for a vacation. I jumped up— my poor hubby was exhausted now. I thought, Lord help us. There is only so much that we can take. All day this boy slams, bangs, and demands and then at night we are on guard too.

For a long time, I stubbornly cared for my son. I never wanted to acknowledge or admit that there would be a day when I could no longer care for him. The world suffering from this pandemic put everything into question for me. I started to openly admit that it was impossible to keep up this pace. It's like when running a marathon—although there are only ten kilometers left in the race, your body becomes tired from all the kilometers that you have already put in. Taking care of Keyan has an exponential effect rather than a cumulative one. The years invested in taking care of him makes it feel as though we have been caring for him for thirty years. I admit I am tired—tired to the core of my being without any end in sight. I do envy all the parents that raise their children and then let them go. I can't wait to see what Manisha is going to do with her life. Keyan, on the other hand, makes me worry—I worry because I know that we cannot take care of him for the rest of our lives. The stress and worry will be the death of us.

I look at the mirror and wonder if I would have aged the same way if Keyan hadn't been autistic. I naturally have black circles under my eyes, but the lack of quality sleep has created a crater effect too—my eyes sunken to the back of my head. This casts a shadow that makes them look darker. I think about what this is doing to my overall health. I know one thing for sure—the stress and lack of sleep have not been kind to my waistline. My hormones have gone wild—especially since turning forty.

Kunal and I are an incredible team. I used to feel we were competing for best parent status. Over time I ceased trying to be. I felt myself going into survival mode. He, being the wonderful man that he is, would always pick up the slack. For the longest time, when he did this, it made me feel less-than, or in other words, inadequate. I had to surrender those feelings because I was overwhelming myself. I could feel that the way I chose to see things was harmful to our relationship. It created a power struggle. As I matured, I could see that it was merely Kunal wanting to take care of his family—he wants to take care of all of us.

I worry about what the lack of sleep is doing to Kunal's health. I feel that we are nearing the end of our capabilities and that we need to confront the future. What does it look like? What would be the best for our family and how do we go about getting there? The good part is that Kunal is a planner. We can't wait until we have nothing left to give our son. We have to prepare for what comes next. Recently we have been talking about a second home so that we can spend time away from Keyan. It would be a place to recharge so that we could take care of him during the week. He would stay home with a caregiver, since home is where he is happiest.

It's hard for me to articulate these thoughts—they do not flow easily. I wonder if it is because of an emotional block. Is it me feeling like a failure, or is it partly denial that this is my life? I want to be able to name it and outline my thoughts and emotions surrounding it. All the trauma work that I have done is giving me the clarity to see things clearly. The struggle remains to find the balance between loving my son and myself. Raising him has been a constant battle. We spend time feeling other people's judgement of him. As his parents, we have battled that narrative, trying to educate anyone that will listen that this boy's life matters. He is here for a reason—he is here to teach us something. The best things in life are born from the hardest things we go through. Keyan has challenged every part of me. He has provided me with life's biggest gifts and hardest challenges.

I am not afraid of being vulnerable. Rather, I fear admitting things to myself—I'm scared that when I do, things will all fall apart. I have been through some real tough stuff, and have always been able to rise above it, but one of my greatest fears is falling apart and not being there for my family. When Keyan was little, there was more support in place. Now, as I look to the future, I need to work on creating a new task force of help. I need a regular reprieve from my son. This has come to the forefront because of

COVID. I fear what it will do to me if he can't go back to school in September; I risk falling into a deep depression. I will have to dig deep into the recesses of my being to find the strength to care for Keyan while Kunal works and Manisha goes back to school. I will have to take pen to paper to map out our future and create a strategy that nurtures all of us—not just Keyan.

When I look back, it is amazing at times how I armoured up and got to work caring for my son, my family, and the organization I had built, all the while forsaking my needs. I lived most of my life in survival mode. Lucky for me it got to a point where it all became too heavy to carry. Utterly exhausted, I had to learn to let go. Instead of obsessing about the future and my fears around it, I focus now on the moment. Living in the moment helps to appease my anxiety about Keyan's future and the lack of services required to help me care for my son.

Doing Things for Himself

The older we get, the more it seems as though time moves faster. I have two adult children. I can't believe that I don't have babies anymore. Lately in my dreams, I find myself revisiting the time when my kids were little. Kids and teens tend to have growth spurts both physically and mentally. Keyan has definitely been on the upswing—implementing new skills that he has learned. It's almost as though he is trying to help me out. I have been feeling overwhelmed from "caregiver burnout," magnified by the pandemic and the fact that I have little alone time. So, out of necessity or out of preservation of my energy, I have been asking him to do more things rather than doing them for him—even though he finds that easier. He has definitely been succeeding in his own small ways, and, like I have said before, there are no ceremonies to celebrate his accomplishments, but we acknowledge them here at home.

- Keyan loves to sit at the kitchen table. I think it's his combination of love for food and proximity to his mama. In the mornings, while he is chowing down on breakfast, I am making his lunch and emptying the dishwasher. Since he showers first thing in the morning, once he has eaten we just have to brush his teeth, dress him, and then he is out the door. He is really good at putting on his clothes, but I have to watch him because when left to himself he consistently puts on his clothing backwards. Some of you might be thinking, Well, just let him. Trust me, there have been days when there is no fight left in me and I figure the teachers will know that on that given day he got dressed himself.

- He has started to let the dog out to do her business. It only took him six years, but finally he is helping with the dog. It's ironic since the back door is only a few feet away from where Keyan sits at the kitchen table. He opens the door again when she is ready to come inside. It's super cute.

- I was in the living room folding laundry when Keyan came running up from the basement. He went to sit at the kitchen table, then quickly bounced up. He went to the bathroom to wash his hands. He had never done this before. Like any mom who has a child on the spectrum, I wondered, why the new behaviour? I snuck up on him and realized that he had dirtied his finger. (To ensure full cleanliness, I use a nail brush, hot water, and soap to get his hands clean.) He was not only connecting the dots of what we wanted him to do, but actually doing it. I often wonder how much of his reluctance is autism, versus teenage attitude.

- He likes to drop his backpack at the front door when he gets home from school. Then he either runs to the basement bathroom to go in peace, or he runs to the closet in the kitchen to fling off his shoes and socks.

I have always assisted him in washing his hands after school. He does just that. Because Keyan is a five second hand washer, I follow behind and try to stretch it to the recommended twenty seconds (as per public health and safety guidelines). I am showing him more "how to" and he seems genuinely interested. When he comes home I am usually in the kitchen preparing his first supper. I leave the door unlocked so he can let himself in. I ask him to retrieve his backpack so I can empty his lunch box. The next habit we have to get him to adopt is to empty the contents of his lunchbox, put away his backpack, wash his hands, and then sit down to his first meal.

- The night time routine changes over time. Right now we are in a phase where he likes to go hang out in his room or watch TV. I like to make the beds and I would say that 90 percent of the time I succeed. So when Keyan goes into his room he does a great job of destroying my efforts. It's expected, so I don't sweat it. When it's time for us to get him settled in for the night we ask him to go pee-pee. It is in that span of time that I straighten out his sheets so that I can get him nice and tucked in for the night. The other night I heard him slamming the drawers. I listened to see what he was getting into. When I peered through the door, he had already put toothpaste on his toothbrush and was brushing his teeth. After so many times of asking him to go pee-pee and then brush his teeth, he was like, "Okay, I got this now. I can do this." I was proud of him. Again, our victories.

In these small acts I can see Keyan's desire to be independent and to do more on his own. This makes me hopeful that he will learn to do simple everyday chores.

Because he doesn't have the capabilities to work outside, learning to help in maintaining the home is huge. In essence, that becomes his work. Most often, we feel valued when we are helping others. My hope is that Keyan will connect to that and want to help me on a daily basis by caring for himself and our home.

The Boston Marathon (2013)

Every day, I pour most of my energy into my family, but keep a little reserve for myself. It is important for me that people know that I am more than a special needs mom. That alone does not define me. I am a woman with my very own hopes and dreams for this life. I wear many hats: woman, daughter, sister, wife, friend, manager, content creator, dreamer, athlete, and president of a charitable organization—although most of these come very naturally to me. I want to talk about me as a "woman" and what has selfishly fulfilled me over the past decade and a half. I was lucky enough to discover running, and over time I became obsessed with it. For anyone who wants to talk about running, my door is always open. I can talk about running for hours and hours. To discuss running is to talk about a passion. My ultimate goal as a runner is longevity—to be the oldest woman to cross the finish line. I can see it now—spectators scratching their heads in disbelief or moved to tears by my shuffle across the finish line.

I want to share my thoughts on being a runner—a marathon runner in particular. I am sharing this with you because as a woman who wears different hats, "athlete" is an important one for me. It is selfishly all mine. It is where I go to clear my head. It is where I go to stay sane. It is where I find a desire to want to live a healthier life. Running has uncovered things about me that I didn't know existed. Running is my yoga, my meditation, and my sacred place. Sometimes we have to remind ourselves to leave the gadgets and gizmos at home and to feel ourselves in our bodies—to look around at the beauty and be thankful for being alive.

My marathon journey is pretty incredible. I ran my very first marathon in 2009 in Montreal because it was important for me to have as many of my family and friends at the finish line as possible. My father was so proud of me that when I went to hug him he started to cry and out of embarrassment he buried his face in the crook of my neck. Overall, I have trained for eleven marathons, but I have reached the finish line nine times. In the harsh winter of 2013 I trained for the Boston marathon. I toed the line to the world's most revered marathon on April 15, 2013. It was an incredibly hard course, and I was suffering. I stopped to see my cheering squad around the twenty-five kilometer marker. I was having a hard time breathing because the built-in bra in my tank top was digging into my chest. I took it off and pinned my race bib to my bra. I kissed my family and friends and off I went.

With merely two hundred meters left of my race, the first of two bombs went off, forcing me off the course. I felt the second bomb go off right behind me. It felt like a terrorist attack. Chaos ensued. People were screaming, "Run! Run for your life!" I was too scared to look back. Panic everywhere. Although things were moving incredibly quickly, it was as though my mind was processing it in slow motion, allowing me the time to make right decisions. All

I wanted to do was to find my family and get out of there. I wanted us to be safe. Luckily, within minutes, I was able to find my family and friends in the family waiting area. I was the one to confirm to them that bombs had gone off and that we needed to vacate the premises ASAP.

The following year, the Boston Athletic Association invited all those who did not cross the finish line in 2013 back again.

I suffered from PTSD and needed to include therapy as part of my training this time. I worked with a psychotherapist, acupuncturist, and osteopath to work on both my body and mind. I was determined to go back and cross the finish line, to feel all the glory of being a Boston marathon finisher. This story was years in the making, starting off with the three marathons it took me to qualify to run Boston. Sadly, crossing the finish line of the 2014 Boston marathon would be bitter-sweet for me. My dad had passed away nineteen days prior to the race. He wouldn't be there to hug me at the finish line like he had done so many times before.

This marathon was more than a running race—it was a show of strength in the face of adversity and proof of my resilience and determination to finish what I had started. I felt my father in spirit. He carried me when I wanted to quit—I was so scared to be near the finish line where the bombs had gone off the year before. I had to convince myself that it was safe to finish the race. When I turned left onto Boylston street and looked in the distance at the finish line, my heart began to race; I thought I was going to have a heart attack. I was so scared. I took a deep breath and reminded myself that I was in good health and that I was safe to finish. Then it was as though the finish line came to me rather than me running to it. Like in a movie. I crossed the finish line overcome with emotions. I wept. I hugged strangers who like me felt the heaviness of coming back from 2013.

I had a few minutes to process what had just happened before falling into my mother's arms—grateful that we both had the strength to come back. All the emotions came pouring out of us in a stream of tears: the loss of my father, the terror we had felt last year, the fear of coming back, and finally—the joy of finishing that which had meant so much to me for so long.

DNF–Did Not Finish

When referring to marathon running, people have said to me, "It's easy for you now because you have run so many." The truth is that it never gets easy. If it was easy, then what would be the glory in doing it? None! When we are at our strongest, we want to run faster and when at our weakest, we simply want to finish the race. In the spring of 2018 I had my first "did not finish" (DNF) of my own doing. It played badly on my self-esteem as a runner. On that day, all I had in me was seventeen kilometers. I fantasized about a volunteer sweeping me off the course and driving me in a golf cart to where I wanted to go. That doesn't happen in a marathon. Wherever you stop, you have to make your own way back. I struggled tremendously, but walk-ran to the twenty-seven kilometer marker where I knew Kunal would be. He did his best to get me back onto the course but I was adamant that my race was over. I never over-analyzed what went wrong. Maybe it was all in my head, but I'll never know. Instead, I choose to feel the negative emotions and then I let go so that I could get on with my life.

The DNF forced me to reset. I reminded myself of why I love running. What running has brought to my life. How running has saved me. Therefore, I am not defined by a DNF. I have to thank my ageing body that, although it is slower now, I am still able to run. There are so many valuable lessons that have come from my running. It has held up a mirror to who I really am, rather than what people perceive me to be. I am incredibly resilient, and when I fall down I know how to get back up. Both my running and my life have reflected that truth. My running has also shown that when I set my mind to do something, I do it. A journey that started off with a bet to run ten kilometres, turned into a desire to run a marathon, and finally turned into a dream of running the Boston marathon. I am proof that when we believe in ourselves, we can do hard things.

MARATHONS
    Montreal marathon, Quebec
    Green Mountain marathon, Vermont
    Hudson Mohawk marathon, Albany
    Ottawa marathon, Ontario
    Hudson Mohawk marathon, Albany (Boston qualified)
    Boston marathon, Massachusetts (2013)
    Boston marathon, Massachusetts
    Vermont City marathon, Vermont
    Ottawa marathon, Ontario (DNF)
    Hudson Mohawk marathon, Albany
    (At last count I had run twenty half-marathons.)

Les Lilas–Marathon

After crossing the finish line at the Montreal marathon I still wasn't happy.
Do you know why?
Well, it's because I ran and I walked.
In essence I saw it as completing a marathon
BUT not running it.
The next year I set out to run a marathon.
On a cold fall morning in South Hero, Vermont,
I crossed the finish line having run a marathon—never walking.
With only my husband and parents to receive me at the finish line I cried—
I was overjoyed
that this girl who was never in her whole life good at sports
was able to accomplish such a feat.

Again the thrill fizzled away because
I wanted to be viewed not only as a runner
but a good runner.
I set my eye on the Boston marathon
which is the holy grail of marathons.
You see you have to qualify for the Boston marathon.

That means run another marathon in a set time in order to make it into Boston.
I was obsessed.
Boston was my unicorn.
AND I wanted it bad.

After I made up my mind that I wanted to run Boston, I qualified on the third try.
I gave my all in that marathon,
bringing myself to the absolute brink of my abilities—
although there are
(and I know people who are) athletically gifted enough to qualify for Boston on their first try.
BUT I am not here to share their story—
I am here to share mine.
I broke down on several occasions the day I qualified for Boston.
The first time was when the pace bunny turned to us and said,
"One mile left to Boston."
At that moment I knew I was going to qualify for Boston.
Little old me had accomplished something I never thought possible.
Finally, I thought to myself I have proven to the whole world that
"I am good enough."
I couldn't believe that this mama bear
who is raising two young children
and one on the autism spectrum
was able to perform such a feat.
I had six months to prepare for Boston.
In those six months I was mindful of everything—
soaking up everything the experience had to offer.
I was totally enamoured with everything Boston.
At the time I was a substitute teacher at a local high school.

I was so excited about having qualified for Boston
that I shared my excitement with my students.
Unlike the adults who surrounded me, they were sincerely interested.
I wanted to teach them that regardless of age
we can plant a seed and nurture it to grow.
What started out as a stress reliever
became a desire for more—
essentially becoming a passion that I never would have imagined.
This didn't happen overnight.
It took me two years to fall head-over-heels madly in love with running.
That passion turned into a DREAM.
It's important to remember that running didn't start off as a PASSION or a DREAM.
It developed over time.

Leading up to the Boston marathon
I invited my family and close friends to make the trip with me.
This was the most exciting thing that had ever happened to me.
Something I had done on my own.
We were a crew of fourteen people.
For the marathon, I bought my family and friends matching green T-shirts
so I could spot them easily on the course
as I passed by.
I have to tell you everything was magical.
That is until I was two hundred meters from the finish line
and the bombs went off.
Everything that transpired after that was terrifying.
I managed to get to my family and friends and make it to safety.

I don't want to go into gross detail about what happened, but let's just say I suffered from post-traumatic stress afterwards.

I worked with a psychologist and acupuncturist to help alleviate the trauma.

The Boston Athletic Association decided that in 2014 they would invite the six thousand

who hadn't crossed the finish line to return.

The opportunity to finish what we started.

It was a hard decision to make but I went back.

Triage Protocol

I was designed to push painful things away. I learned to numb myself to them and block hurtful things from my memory. It's a defence mechanism. Growing up, that is how I processed pain. Then I became a mom and things changed. The old defence mechanism I had built for numbing no longer worked. Having children changed me and it also changed my brain. I had to learn to process, feel, and retain all of it to protect my kids. That is when the ferocious protector inside of me emerged and a mama bear was born.

During the height of the pandemic, the Quebec government adopts a triage protocol that will deny individuals with special needs access to ICU care and ventilators in the event of a second wave of COVID-19. For most people, it doesn't apply. But it applies to Keyan, and I am devastated. This is where I struggle as a mom and an autism advocate. I feel that those who care are those who are directly affected. I begin to feel the isolation of our struggles.

Stepping Away

It is an act of courage to walk away from things that no longer serve us. We often find comfort and security in what is familiar, so we stay stuck, even when the situation or relationship has to come to an end. COVID made me take a hard look at things and forced me to make some very difficult decisions. I had to walk away from toxic relationships and my people-pleasing ways. At first, I worried about what everyone would think, but that way of thinking wasn't going to help me in any way. I had to make some changes.

I could not have imagined how 2020 was going to play out. Instead of continuing to fight an already extremely tough battle, I got wise enough to back down. The decade-long fight had knocked me to my knees and I couldn't see a way of getting up. I saw the lockdown in March as an opportunity to ask the hard questions. Did I want to take S.Au.S. to the next level, and was I willing to continue sacrificing my life for others? No, I got tired of being invisible. People will see what they want to see, and so I always wondered if they saw how hard it was. Did they care that I was on the verge of a breakdown? If

I walked away, would they notice? Why was I still here? I realized that my heart started the journey, but along the way my ego took over. I had wanted to prove that I was good enough, smart enough, and determined enough to make real change. I could have achieved my goals, but in order to do so, I would have had to work closely with the government, and I never wanted to do that. In my experience, all the government seems to do is get in its own way with lots of bureaucratic red tape, constantly slowing things down. Towards the end, it felt as though everyone was looking at me rather than working with me. It felt lonely doing the work. My therapist often talks about leaders and visionaries being lonely people because they have the vision that others around them don't. When he would say that, I would think to myself, I don't want this, these feelings of loneliness, isolation, and not being heard. I felt invisible.

Have you ever been in a room surrounded by people and felt totally alone? I have, more than I would like to admit. That's how I felt anytime I was in a meeting with the S.Au.S. Board of Directors, the government, corporate leaders, and even parents of autistic children. The feelings of isolation paired with being misunderstood began to wear me down. When I started this work I pushed those feelings down as far as I possibly could, all in the name of activism. I didn't see any of my feelings as valid, so I learned to ignore them to serve the greater good. The autism community needed me, so I sacrificed myself to get the job done—until I couldn't anymore. It became harder for me to keep it together once the projects got bigger. It was taking a serious toll on me. I had made sacrifices of time, money, and energy over the years, and I was feeling the side effects now. I had become extremely tired, stressed, and frustrated with the work and all it demanded from me. I was on the verge of burnout.

With the cancellation in 2020 of the Autism Awareness Run and the gala I knew it was the time for me to call it. A journey that started in 2009 would end for me in 2020 because of the pandemic, paired with total burnout. Leaving the organization would allow me to carve out a whole new life for myself, focusing on the things that mattered most—my husband, my daughter, and my son.

June 16, 2020

Attn: To the Board of Directors of S.Au.S.

It has been an honour and a privilege to serve as President of the Board of Directors-S.Au.S. I am extremely proud of the work that has been accomplished over the years. Albeit, there is still a long road ahead. I trust that with the right president and board members, the organization will elevate to the next level. The goal of creating programs for adults with level three autism will in fact become a reality with the right group of individuals at the helm.

I believe those with more experience, knowledge, and contacts will be better suited for the position. We need to breathe new life into the organization by broadening our reach and it is my firm belief that this can only be accomplished by my stepping down as President of the BOD.

As I mentioned in our meeting dated October 28, 2019, it was my intention to step down as president in order to take better care of my son. I need to ensure that all measures are in place when he transitions from adolescent to young adult (eighteen years old). This process can be long and daunting, and therefore, needs to be executed with care.

I have dedicated many years of my life to the autism community and will continue to do so but in a different role. To ensure continuity, I am proposing to stay on as a volunteer in a modified role as Director of Public Relations, continuing to build relationships with government, communities, and other organisations. It is important to me to stay in a major decision making role (in operations) so that the overall integrity of S.Au.S. is maintained. This journey began in 2009 with a glorious Autism Awareness Run in Parc Montcalm and I remain dedicated to doing my part to ensure its continued success.

I want to thank all of you for your support and trust you understand that I need to do this for my family, myself, and the greater good.

Thank you,
Audrey Burt

My North Star

My teacher—this person right here has been my biggest teacher.
Over the past three months he has taught me what I need to focus on.
He has asked me to turn inward and ask the hard questions.
The time has come to no longer give away my time, energy, love, and support.
I must preserve it—for him, myself, and my whole family, where my love and loyalty lies.
Life is too short and too precious to deny ourselves.
Keyan has forced an awakening within me that I have been denying for a long time.
I can no longer hide behind my fear of the future—his future and our future.
His guidance goes beyond the spoken word.
Rather, he holds up a mirror.
He asks us all to take a long hard look.
What do you see?

The task was daunting but necessary.
Thank you, world, for slowing things down so that I could figure things out.

For those who look at our lives and wonder, "How does he feel? How does she do it?"—
the answer is LOVE.
My profound love for my son gives me strength and helps me to rise up.
The love he has for me makes him feel safe and always at home.
I would like to take a moment to thank my son, my teacher, my guide, and my heart—for showing me that so many things are possible.
Without you, I don't know where I would be.

Our curly hair babe receives his diagnosis at eighteen months old.

Our little family
celebrating Keyan's
second birthday.

Manisha cheers me on
at my first ten kilometer
run (Sept. 2006).

Keyan at the inaugural
Autism Awareness Run
in 2009.

Manisha reciting her
slam poem at an S.Au.S.
gala to a room of four
hundred people.

Smiles at Camp Oasis.

Cuddling with Keyan is
my favourite.

Taking a moment at the 2014 Boston Marathon to acknowledge my family and friends who have come to cheer me on.

One of the greatest honours bestowed on me. Proud that my work is being acknowledged by my country.

My last marathon—
Albany, NY (October
2019.)

My loves, my life,
my little teachers.

Papa and Keyan riding tandem.

Keyan walking his service dog, Bagou.

A glimpse into our future. Days spent in peace and harmony.

Getting ready to do some bead work.

A family selfie at the cottage (July 2020).

PART III

Awakening to Peace and Harmony

Les Lilas–Allow Me to Reintroduce Myself

My name is Audrey Burt.
I stand before you a forty-six-year-old woman—
a wife,
mother,
daughter, sister,
and friend.
I am the president and founder of a charitable organization.
I am a runner.
And I wanna be a triathlete.

It's hard as moms to give ourselves permission to do things that fulfill us.
We have been raised to think that to be a good mom we have to sacrifice our happiness.
Good mothers put themselves last. Right?!
That couldn't be further from the truth.
I became the best mom when I was advocating for my son;
I was able to provide him with what he needed to thrive.
And at the same time I became a role model for my daughter.
She saw that whatever came my way, I wouldn't give up.
If you think moms to normal kids put themselves last,

you can only imagine what the mom to a "special needs" child goes through.

It took me years of taking baby steps—ten kilometers, half marathon, marathon, to Boston—to allow myself permission to do what I needed to do and still oftentimes I felt guilt.

My husband was also part of the guilt equation (the belief that good moms are martyrs).

You know it's not because someone says something that makes it true—

you have to internalize and repeat it over and over like a mantra—

I am deserving of happiness—

I am worthy of fulfillment.

Joy

There have been moments of happiness worked hard for
and achieved.
A medal when crossing a finish line—or even a degree.
I have learned that we chase happiness, but
"joy" is more profound,
because it's in the simple and mundane
things—uncovered to be found.
Joy is solitude when things slow down.
The chirp of a bird,
a majestic garden,
and the glow of snow, on the ground.
Joy is personal.
No expectations, kudos, or with anyone else around.
My joy has been revealed through self-compassion and
love abound.
This may sound corny, simple, or absurd.
BUT,
I find joy in this moment
with my feet firmly planted on the ground.
The simple act of putting
thoughts to paper—
to stop them from swirling around.

Rest, Run, and Write

It is said that we are put on this earth for a reason, and I strongly feel as though I have found my reason. From the moment Keyan was diagnosed with autism, my life changed in so many ways. I had to listen to what the universe was telling me. By listening and paying close attention, I learned that instead of always fighting, sometimes it's better to surrender and take the path of least resistance.

When Keyan was little, I remember being tired to the core of my being. Every muscle was aching and every thought was negative; I would fantasize about what it would be like to escape my life—escape the dark cloud of autism (a disorder that dictated my days and nights). An aha moment—why not go away for a week? Time away from the children would help me recharge and get out of my negative haze. I proposed the idea to Kunal, whose swift response was that we couldn't leave Keyan. I let him know that I was going on vacation for a week and that the only thing he had to decide was whether or not he would be joining me. I was so desperate to escape. My husband reluctantly jumped on board and we put a team together to care for the children. We packed up and went on an all-inclusive vacation to the Dominican Republic. It was one of the best decisions that I ever made! In that one week the heaviness started to leave my body, I connected with my husband on a deeper level, and best of all I missed my kids so much that it gave me renewed energy to face the challenges when I got back.

In many ways that vacation made it clear to me that it was important that Kunal and I do things for ourselves. One of the heaviest burdens we carry as parents to a child with special needs is that we feel, in those moments that we are not caring for our child(ren), that we are taking away from them. Think about it, our children need us so much in their day-to-day lives, how could we selfishly take away from them? The irony is that when we take care of our own needs, we are mentally, physically, and emotionally stronger to care for our children. As parents, we sometimes hold on too tight for too long, then realize that our children can do things that we hadn't given them space to do. Even a special needs child, as they grow, needs to be surrounded by individuals outside of the family circle; they need personal space despite loving the hugs and kisses, and like everyone else they need some alone time. So it is in those moments that parents can take the time to read, exercise, take a long bath, go out for dinner, attend a concert, or do whatever their hearts desire. As our special needs child ages, oftentimes we go from being a parent to a caregiver, and in that role it is even more vital to not only take time for self-care but to ensure that there is more time for self-care in the future.

My self-care has come in the form of running. Running was how I took care of myself. It made me a much happier and healthier person and therefore a better mom. My running journey has been a magical one, from running on dirt roads in Vermont alongside cows in a pasture, to city streets. Running is like meditating for me.

Running gave me the courage to do things that I never thought would be possible. The more I challenged myself in running, the more I challenged myself in other spheres of my life. I could never have imagined the gifts that running would bring into my life. I had manifested running the Boston marathon the year I turned forty. To celebrate turning forty-five, I participated in Ironman 70.3 in Mont-Tremblant. Nothing could have taken me further outside of my comfort zone than to swim in a murky lake, cycle down steep hills, and then finish it off with a half-marathon run. When I crossed that finish line, it felt as though I had won the race.

Throughout the years I have religiously used the morning to write. As a form of self-care, akin to therapy, I write down my thoughts, feelings, and experiences. Putting pen to paper makes me feel as though I am writing a song. When I am typing on my computer, I am playing the piano. It is me writing my song, "Living in Tandem." To mark my fiftieth birthday (January 9, 2023), I will celebrate the upcoming release of this book. It is my gift to myself, my family, and my readers.

Discovering Growth

Due to COVID, we hadn't been anywhere outside of our home for months, so I decided to reserve a quaint cottage directly on Lac des Français, in the Rawdon area, about an hour and fifteen minutes from home. It was meant to be a weekend away as a family and a change of scenery. Most importantly, it was a gift to highlight Kunal's upcoming fiftieth birthday. A weekend away, cocooned as a family. One of Kunal's favourite things is spending time as just the four of us. Instead of having a big party to highlight Kunal turning fifty, I planned and organized individual or small group dates with family and friends.

Our good friends have a cottage on the same lake, so we planned to leave the kids for a few hours to enjoy a lovely dinner at their place. This was booked over a month in advance and I was really looking forward to spending time with one of our favourite couples. When we're together we have the best time. We catch up on life and spend lots of time laughing.

I challenged myself to pack without getting anxious or frustrated. I rarely work myself up when I am packing for myself, but it's a different story when it's for the whole family. There is the pressure of forgetting things. Other travel necessities that need to be packed are the layers of bedding that Keyan requires. Because of his continued bedwetting, we travel with a plastic mattress cover, a rubber bath mat, sheets, blankets, and his own pillow. Yes, you read that correctly, we carry a rubber bath mat, the kind you put at the bottom of the tub to ensure you don't slip. It serves as an extra layer of protection for the mattress. When Keyan pees the bed, it can sometimes be from head to toe so we need to take all precautions.

I decided to keep Keyan home from school instead of picking him up mid-day for our departure. The day before, he had had a bad day at school and I was asked to pick him up early. His teacher had been out for a couple of days, then his educator was absent for a few more. Clearly it was too much change for his brain to process and accept. Their absence came after I had been away for a three-night getaway in Bromont. That had been a desperately needed escape to rest my tired body and over-stimulated mind. The absence of his go-to people sent Keyan spiralling. It had been too much change at once. I decided that it was better to keep Keyan home with me before leaving for the cottage to help him recover from what had been a stressful week for him.

I needed to go to the grocery store so I decided it would be perfect to take Keyan for a drive, since he loves being in the car and I wanted him to start the weekend off happy. I got the groceries for the weekend and he waited in the car. The next stop was the pharmacy because I forgot my razor in Bromont and I felt like a Sasquatch. When I came out of the pharmacy I saw that he had something in his hands and he was chewing. What did he have? Raw cookie dough. He found the roll of Pillsbury dough cookies and was going to town on it. You know what it feels like when a toddler drops the f-bomb? It's not funny but in fact it's really funny. That is how I felt. I was literally in the pharmacy for three minutes, tops, and he managed to rummage through the groceries to find something to eat. When I got to him, there was only half of the roll of cookie dough left in his hands; I proceeded to confiscate it. He didn't complain, so I assumed that he had had his fill.

When we got home, I baked the remaining cookies, and Keyan headed downstairs to nap. The sky was grey and the overall feeling was somber, the perfect day to bundle up and sleep. Keyan proceeded to take a two-hour nap, which was unusual for him. I strongly believe that he knows what he needs for his body, so I let him sleep. When he woke up, Kunal took him to shower. We were one step closer to leaving, so I started packing the car—but something was off. The strangest thing happened. After showering, Keyan came downstairs, but he didn't go to the kitchen table which we had expected him to do since he had slept through lunch. This is a boy who loves to eat, so when he doesn't want to eat we are left wondering, "What is going on?" He was back downstairs in the basement signalling to us that he wanted to be alone. It was obvious to me that he was not feeling well, so I decided to give him Advil. He spilled half of the liquid Advil on his shirt and jumped up; after running upstairs he now wanted to go outside into the spa. I felt discouraged because the rest of us were packed and excited; we were about to hit the road.

I thought, If I give him ten minutes in the spa, then we can go. Kunal, on the other hand, didn't want Keyan to go into the spa, because unbeknownst to me, he had just put in the chemicals. Keyan was determined. A battle of wills was playing out in front of me and tensions were high. I said nothing. It was all a delicate dance. Kunal told Keyan not to go into the spa and wrangled him into the car. I was feeling sick to my stomach over what was transpiring, so I withdrew until it was time to go. When Kunal, the more patient of us two, begins to lose patience, it automatically forms a knot in the pit of my stomach. Why? Because it usually doesn't end well. Once in the car, it took us a few minutes to decide on the best route to take. According to Google maps, there was a ton of traffic everywhere. With my stress level running high, and Keyan's combative mood, I strongly made a stance to avoid the Lafontaine Tunnel. I have a phobia of tunnels, and the thought of being bumper to bumper with the potential of my autistic son having a meltdown was overwhelming. I strongly encouraged Kunal to take another route. At first he was very hesitant, but I was grateful that he could sense my distress and he agreed to take an alternate route. I could breathe more easily.

We got going, and before long we were slowly moving on Route 132 between traffic lights. I thought to myself, We should have taken the A-30. I said nothing, because the tension in the car was so high. Energetically, I was losing it—experiencing all kinds of feelings. I talked to myself in an attempt to become anchored. It felt as though I was going to lose it at any minute. We got onto the Mercier Bridge and things were moving, only to get to the other side where we were once again bumper to bumper. Keyan was showing signs of frustration. He needs to constantly be moving in the car or he becomes agitated. He was banging his fist into his thigh and hitting the car door. Both Kunal and I were overwhelmed by Keyan's fragility and feared that something bad might happen. We didn't admit it to each other, but I know that we were both fearing the worst case scenarios: Keyan breaking the window, bloodying his hand, and needing urgent care; or becoming aggressive to the point of hurting Manisha; or somehow getting out of the car and running into traffic. The likelihood of these things happening are slim, but I know they still take up space in the dark recesses of our imagination. We fear things escalating to the point of other people getting involved. This would only make matters worse. In these situations, because I can't offer to drive the car, I need to support Kunal in every way that I can. I am a good copilot. I highlight the route to take and offer snacks, drinks, and music selection. On a long trip, I tell stories and download music or podcasts. When Keyan is onboard, I know to avoid both turning back to make eye contact and talking too much because he prefers peace.

Kunal pressed a finger into the skin of my leg to get my attention. He said, "What do you think if we just turn back and go home?" According to the map, there were still several traffic hotspots ahead on the route to get to the cottage. He said we could leave later that night or first thing in the morning. I agreed immediately, because the energy of it all was too much for any of us to handle. Only Manisha was at peace, asleep in the backseat. I was grateful for this. I loved that there were times when she missed out on the tension. As soon as I said, "Yes," Kunal got out of the traffic lane and headed towards the Champlain Bridge; I instantly felt better and the tension began to melt away.

Usually we would feel like failures for not having reached our destination. There would be a quiet resentment towards Keyan for having ruined our plans. The truth is that autism has taught us that we need to be flexible in order to meet Keyan's needs. His rigidity forces us to be extremely flexible in our expectations. I had envisioned us buzzing around, exploring our cottage rental, grateful to finally be somewhere other than home. But here we were, turned back around to sit within our four walls. The irony is that I was happy simply because Keyan was calm, the tension was gone, and we were all safe. Tomorrow would be a new day, and I would much rather travel when everyone was feeling good and there was no extra stress to deal with.

As soon as we got back home, Keyan ate and then immediately jumped into the spa. A kind of f-you to his papa for not allowing him to go in earlier. I wondered whether giving him the time to jump in earlier would have enabled us to make it to our destination. We would never know. He stayed in the spa for a long time. I started to get hungry, so I whipped out the ingredients I had purchased to make a charcuterie board. A simple but delicious supper. Kunal lit a fire. We sat fireside, enjoying a glass of wine and the safety of our home. I couldn't get warm even sitting right next to the fire. My body told me that I needed a good soak. I headed upstairs to take a detox bath in hopes that it would regulate my body temperature and wash away the stress of the day. Afterwards, I summoned Kunal to take a long walk—just the two of us. I felt it was important that we spent time alone to digest the emotions of the day. We agreed to wake early and head out on our second attempt at the cottage. We wanted to get there as early as possible to enjoy the day and whatever the surroundings had to offer.

The weekend didn't start off the way we wanted it to, with us now having lost $250 on the missed night. In the past, we would have labelled our weekend a failure. Instead, we now saw the weekend as a huge win. We were learning to let go of things—of expectations. The biggest takeaway was Kunal's willingness to put our mental and physical well-being above all else. In the past, Kunal would have been determined to execute our plans at all cost (I am still trying to figure out where his stubbornness comes from), but during the pandemic we were reminded of what mattered most. It felt like we were being tested in this situation, and we passed with flying colours.

Manifesting My Life

As a little girl, I dreamed about the life I would one day have. More than anything, I wanted to be married and have children. My focus was more on the children rather than the husband part, though I envisioned building a life with a man who would provide emotional and financial stability. My education was also important to me—I really wanted a university education. I knew that a formal education would elevate me beyond living paycheque to paycheque. I came from a blue collar family and my parents always struggled financially. I didn't want to struggle like they had. There were so many parts of my childhood that I did not want to bring into my adult life.

I was extremely blessed to have met a fantastic guy early on in life—the hard part was holding onto him. I was only fifteen years old when Kunal and I met. We drifted apart for a few months, but found our way back to one another. I went away for cegep and decided that a long distance relationship would be too hard. I broke it off with Kunal. Yes, he was heartbroken, but the fear in the pit of my stomach was bigger than me. I thought, I don't want to wake up one day having only been intimate with one person and then feeling like I had missed out. What if I married Kunal, then at forty years old regretted not having explored other relationships? I could see myself in that scenario having a mid-life crisis. I would wake up at forty years old, find myself married with kids, and then wonder what I had missed out on. Would I blame it on the fact that I had never explored the world beyond us? I was so young and adventurous, and although I loved Kunal, I needed to know for sure that there was no other one for me.

After two semesters I came back to Montreal to live with my grandparents and that meant that I was back with Kunal. Now that the distance gap was closed and I had indeed dated someone else while away, it felt right for Kunal and I to get back together. The whole time I was away at school we never lost touch. I knew Kunal was the love of my life because he never gave up on us. Once we got back together we constantly had conversations about what we wanted out of life—big picture stuff—and we wanted the same things.

Before getting married, I made it perfectly clear that I didn't want a career, but to be a stay at home mom. We talked about having a large family. I would raise the children and he would focus on his career. I remember with a pride-filled heart how successful he was in his upward trajectory. He didn't have it easy, but his determination to provide for us was unwavering and still is to this day, over thirty years later. It's amazing the number of sleepless nights he endured because of Keyan, and he was still able to have a successful career.

I often find myself counting my blessings, and honestly believe that with all the hours I spent as a little girl, daydreaming of the life that I have now, that I was the one who manifested it. I manifested getting an education, marrying a good man, having children, and having a beautiful home filled with love. I continue to manifest. As a young adult, I said I wanted to drive an Acura MDX, live in a Pottery Barn catalogue, and wear Ralph Lauren. I drive a Lexus truck (this became my preferred vehicle), my house is designed with West Elm pieces (Pottery Barn's sister company), and I prefer White House Black Market. As a more mature adult, I envision using my time to do good. I want to find ways to use my voice and to help those in need. The desire to help others is an innate quality that I have. As a little girl I knew that one day people would know me. I had hoped that it would be for my singing voice, but instead it came in the form of an activist voice. Even as a small child I had wanted to make an impression on the world. I had wanted to matter. I had wanted to make a difference and I succeeded in doing that by building a successful charitable organization that services the autism community. I continue to dream of my future. I look to find gentler ways to care for myself, my family, and others.

Peace is what I value most. When I think of my future now, it is time spent where things are still and quiet. I picture myself with Kunal walking in our country home. Our very own sanctuary of peace. We have figured out how to care for Keyan but also how to spend time away from him. Although I don't know how the future will play out, this is how I envision it and what I hope to manifest once again.

Les Lilas–Plant the Seed

I have always been a firm believer in taking baby steps—
runners who believe in this approach will say,
"Slow and steady wins the race."
It's like planting a garden.
If you plant too many seeds at once
and too close together
they will suffocate.
Your attention has to be on
one seed at a time.
If you want to plant a seed for yourself—
say you want to better your health,
make more time for yourself,
take up a hobby (whether that be learning a new language,
knitting, or wood carving),
participate in a sport,
volunteer, or
write a book—
then focus on that seed
and nurture it.
It's best to plant other seeds farther apart.
You want to construct a solid foundation before you
continue to build.

You see, planting too many seeds can be overwhelming, and you want to stay focused for the best outcome.

I think I will start with a seed I planted more than twelve years ago (the Autism Awareness Run).
The message I want all of you to leave with is the following:
for every action there is a reaction–Sir Isaac Newton.
What I want you to see is that every step you take,
however "small,"
has the potential to grow.
And it will grow to wherever you are willing to take it.
See, a woman is a force to be reckoned with,
and when she sets her mind to something and gives it her time, love, and energy,
it can lead to a PASSION or develop into a DREAM.

Take a seed for example.
They are so itty bitty.
A seed on its own is nothing.
But when it is planted in rich soil–
provided water and sunlight–
it will grow.
It will grow into a beautiful flower, delicious fruit or vegetable, or even a tree.
The seed which becomes a plant is still
fragile and delicate as it grows.
But if it's cared for,
it has a better chance to not only survive
but to thrive.

Your action is the seed
(the thing you want to do–the thing you would like to pursue).
And your desire to be a good gardener
(the steps you take to fulfill that)

will help the plant grow.

Let me put it to you this way—
you have to decide what you want out of life!!!
What do you want your life to look like?
You have to take the steps to create it.
If you sit around waiting for life to happen
you will be utterly disappointed.
That's not how it works.
You have to take action—you have to plant the seed.

Soldiering On

The kids, my husband, the house, the job, self-care, personal projects—a never ending "to do list" that never seems to get done. When I am sick or lack motivation, sometimes borderline depressed, I have no choice but to soldier on. That is what a mama bear does. Oftentimes it feels like my words of despair fall on deafened ears. Why is that? Because no one wants to see a strong person fall apart. If I fall apart, what does that mean for everyone else?

If mom falls apart, we no longer have our rock. The one who schedules, cooks, cleans, drives, soothes, listens, advises, and cares. What the hell will that look like for me? She no longer has the strength, because she has been stretched too thin. Yet, she soldiers on—meetings with the school, supper on the table, groceries despite not knowing what to eat, changing wet sheets, making lunches, sure the kids need to get to where they need to go. Ahh—no energy left for self-care. Oh well, I am sure that if I eat the whole cake I'll feel better about things.

I eat the cake—crap, I feel worse. I beat myself up. Take

a shower and you'll feel better. The phone rings—it's the orthodontist to change the appointment. The new hire at work is questionable. Did I make the right call? The husband comes home with his baggage from the day. I listen but truly am not interested because I can't focus.

I had a day from hell but no one wants to hear it. We have to head out to put gas in the car and drive the kids to their activities. But wait, don't you hear me? Don't you see me? I am struggling. The children come first. I am being pushed and pulled in all directions. I don't think I can do this much longer. Oh, I tell myself, tomorrow is a new day. Soldier on because I have no choice.

The next morning comes. It starts off with exhaustion because my body is not ready to wake. I pray that my morning coffee will make it all better. The kids don't want to get up and now we are rushing. I feel the pulse of the day rising. I push those feelings down because the kids come first.

Get dressed for a very important ten o'clock meeting, which ends up being a waste of time. I am deflated. Put up a good front for the employees because I set the tone, just like at home. I try, but slowly things keep coming at me. Take a break. The phone rings and I have to rush to school to pick up my son because it's not going well. His anxiety is a ten out of ten. Breathe. I am a nervous wreck, and because of it I don't want to drive—but I do it anyway because my son needs me.

Get home and start making supper. I don't even want to look at food but I have to feed my children. I try my best to smile around them. I don't want them to feel my stress— my desperation. I force myself to eat so that my children won't pick up on my emotions. I have managed to make it through the day and the night settles in.

I am emotionally exhausted but no one can change that reality. Maybe a warm bath, tea, and a book will help calm me. I try, but I don't even like tea. I haven't been able to calm my brain all day. Now I look forward to bedtime, hoping for reprieve. I pray for a good night's sleep. I know I am kidding myself but I try. The usual middle of the night wake up happens and it's 3 a.m. Thoughts in my head are spinning, telling me tomorrow will be more of the same, but I have to push forward—push through. This is how I have been feeling lately, but it's normal. Why? Because I am a "mama bear." This story is not uniquely mine. I share it with mothers all over the world—we struggle but we soldier on.

Self Regulating

I was having a hard time regulating my nervous system. I didn't know if it was lack of energy, fatigue, emotional hangover, alcohol, or all of it. My thoughts were racing and I was all over the place. I didn't know where to start. I felt like I was spinning out of control. I knew I didn't want to spend my day this way. I thought about writing and meditating for a bit, because that usually helps. I was consumed by self-deprecating thoughts. I knew it was my inner child screaming for attention, and I decided to be patient and kind with her. Today, with focus on loving kindness and compassion, I would overcome these feelings. I decided not to go to the gym because I needed to be away from other people. I cocooned at home instead.

There are times when we need to be our own nurturer. The sun was shining and maybe later I could go for a walk, get fresh air, and still my mind. It wouldn't be good for me to wait until the evening, but rather I would put myself first and walk in the sunshine. I would grant myself the freedom to bounce from activity to activity, and when I got exhausted from it I would go to grounding—meditation and self-care. It was as though I would have to allow the hyper side of me to bounce. Once I got tired and fed up with that, I would calm down. I would have laundry to fold, things to read, or a walk to take. I would have to trust that I will not spend my whole day like this.

I have the power to self-soothe and to stop the voice in my head from being so cruel. If I have to take a midday nap to turn it all off, so be it.

I could take time today to start wrapping Christmas gifts or writing out cards. There was my bedroom Christmas tree to put up. I felt everything calling to me, but I had no desire to do anything. I hated feeling this way—feeling like I couldn't get a grip. I needed to practice non-attachment as taught in Buddhism. Nothing needed my attention. The things I was trying to accomplish didn't need me, or they could at least wait until my heart was in it. Energetically, it would be best to wrap gifts when love was flowing freely, because energy can be passed on that way.

This makes me think of the energy exchange that Keyan and I have always had. When he was little, I would hold him tight and smell his hair. It is as though I was breathing in his light and his energy. With me holding him tight, he felt me and the profound love that I had for him. Even now, every time he gets out of the shower, I swaddle him tight in his towel and pull him close to me. He puts his face in the crook of my neck and I hold him tight. Sometimes we sway side to side. This is our love practice. At this moment I am giving him love, grounding him, and reminding him with my body language that he is loved. At times I think I need this more than he does.

A Child's Love

One of the most incredible things about having children is the unconditional love that comes along with it. To think that there are humans on this planet who love me above all else is an incredible feeling. That love never wavers or wanes. This love is not in the doing but just in the being. Whether I spend the day running around at warp speed or lying in my bed all day, at the end of it, Manisha and Keyan's love for me is the same. I never knew a love like this existed. I often felt the love I received was based on what I did, rather than just on who I am.

The pandemic had me in my head. I spent time questioning the things that I had always believed to be true. As moms, we do so many things for our families, and I wonder what happens when we stop doing them? Does that mean they love us less? Part of me thought, Maybe. If I stop cooking, will I be viewed as less? If I decide to leave the beds unmade once in a while, will I be considered lazy? Will those things correlate to less love? Hell no! It sounds crazy, but part of me feared yes. Being home together as a family and giving myself permission to do less on the days that I didn't have it in me, was paramount to my well-being. I had to surrender the supermom persona, and that was scary to me. The most beautiful thing came from this. I moved away from thinking that people loved me conditionally (based on the things I did for them), to knowing that there was unconditional love in my life.

I let go of a lifelong belief. I let go of the false narrative that had been programmed into me. We are not loved based on what we do, but rather because of who we are.

To My Daughter

My daughter is the epitome of grace. She has grown up alongside of a brother who needs a lot of our attention on a day-to-day basis. He has never been able to play with her, share with her, or support her. He has always kinda just been there taking up space and it is she who has always done for him. Manisha's innate grace has made it so that she accepts her brother for who he is. She understands that as a family, we are a team, and we have to be there for each other.

Manisha has always been sensitive to my emotions. She has been a constant support for me and for all of us. As she said in the slam poem, "I care that my parents will never hear their son say I love you—so I repeat it more than I mean it to spare their pain." She is that person: empathetic, nurturing, intelligent, funny, and independent. Manisha is one of the best human beings that I know, and to call her daughter is an honour and a privilege.

Raising both a neurotypical and a neurodivergent child in tandem is a very delicate dance. We risk messing up because of all the time, energy, and care that is given to our special needs child. This can potentially lead to low self-esteem or low self-worth in the other child. Feelings of inadequacy or of not being good enough are at a higher risk. I have been hyper-aware of these things and so I have worked extra hard to ensure Manisha's overall well-being.

Dear Manisha,

Because of you, I have always strived to be the best that I can be—desperately wanting to be the mom you deserve. It is a misconception that I created S.Au.S. solely for your brother. In fact, I did it for you, too. I wanted to show you that albeit life is hard, we can always dream, think outside the box, and move towards our goals. Life is a gift that should be lived to the fullest even when things don't go according to plan. You, my dear daughter, are the best of both your papa and me: intelligent, empathetic, sarcastic, defiant, adventurous, and fearless. As a young adult, you have shouldered me through some rough patches, reminding me that it is okay to be vulnerable and to lean on you. You remind me that all the things I want for you, I should want for myself too—the freedom to live life unapologetically. I want you to go out and live the biggest and fullest life that you can. You mean the world to me. You are my light in the darkness. You make me brave and it is because of you that I found the courage to write this book.

Thank you will never be enough for all the gifts you have given me.

With all my love - mama bear - xox

Grace

My father fought a nine-month battle with cancer and passed away in April 2014. Anyone who has watched a loved one battle this horrid disease knows firsthand the toll that it takes on the family's health and emotional state. I had such a hard time with my father being sick that it was essential to my well-being that I find an outlet for my grief. It didn't matter how much I cried, ate, or drank—the hole in the pit of my stomach never filled. The gaping hole inside of me was sadness, and nothing but the space to grieve and time would heal it. I needed some sort of guidance. I turned to Buddhism. I picked up the book FEAR: *Essential Wisdom for Getting Through the Storm* by the famous Buddhist monk, Thich Nhat Hanh. I read the passages of this book over and over again and it soothed my fears. He made me understand that my father was always going to be with me; his energy would survive even after his physical body was gone. I found comfort in that. Honestly, this book is what kept me going.

Out of all religions, Buddhism seems the most natural to me. I jokingly call myself a virgin Buddhist. In essence, if I had a desire to follow any type of religion, it would be

Buddhism. I practice yoga, meditate, and read Buddhist writings but never consistently.

After my father's passing I wanted to do something to honour him and so I decided to get my first tattoo. Although my father and I were as different as night and day, we loved each other deeply. My father made me crazy, but still he pushed me to be the woman I am today (thanks for that Dad). The desire for his constant approval always made me want to do more—to do better. In the same year of his passing, on his birthday, I got the tattoo. It was to honour his life and, in some way, to carry him with me every day thereafter. I decided on a small lotus flower, sparked by the book by Thich Nhat Hanh.

When I was deciding on what type of tattoo to get, I had to think long and hard because of its permanence. The symbolism of the lotus flower resonated with me. Choosing a lotus flower to represent my father seemed absolutely absurd. When I described the tattoo to my siblings, they were utterly confused. What they didn't know was how much the principles found in Buddhist teachings had helped me to cope with our father's illness. The lotus flower represents peace and tranquillity. It represents that very difficult time in my life. Ironically, my father was abrasive and rough around the edges, the total opposite of the zen nature of the lotus flower. I think an anchor would have represented him better as the old school macho kind of guy.

The lotus flower represents, for me, my father's passing. But its significance has an even deeper meaning. The lotus flower also represents the other important males in my life: my husband, my son, and my father-in-law. Kamal (my father-in-law) means lotus flower. Kunal means lotus, too, and Nalik (Keyan's middle name in the feminine) also means lotus flower. The lotus flower therefore represents all the strong male figures in my life. The symbolism of the lotus flower was absolutely something I could permanently wear on my body.

It didn't take long before I wanted another tattoo. When a dear friend told me that she was going to get her long awaited tattoo, I took it as a sign. We would go together. I had "GRACE" tattooed on my wrist, directly below the lotus flower. Grace is Manisha's middle name. Over time, when I was asked about why I had the lotus flower tattooed on my wrist, I would feel guilty that Manisha was not part of its meaning. How could I leave out one of the most important people in my life? What kind of message was that sending to Manisha? I feared that she thought it was because somehow she wasn't important or didn't matter—and nothing could be further from the truth. I was determined to right my wrong.

I have always loved the name Grace and I was inspired to give it to Manisha as a middle name because of the band U2. They had released an album entitled *All That You Can't Leave Behind*. I fell in love with the song "Grace" and would listen to it on repeat. The line, "Grace, it's a name for a girl—it's also a thought that, changed the world," says that it is both her name and a state of being. To live in grace is to be good, kind, and generous. I wanted to carry both my daughter's name and the reminder to live this life in grace.

Pandora's Box

Life can be overwhelming and because of that, our desire to tune out is huge. We want to numb our pains and forget how hard it all can be. We miss contributing to our own lives by over-consuming, be it with social media, food, drink, or something else.

As I reflected on why I love creating content, I realized that it was not only because I got to share my life (often demystifying autism), but also because I got a hit of dopamine from the likes. There was a time when admitting this brought me an incredible amount of shame. I was embarrassed to admit that I sought approval from others—external validation was my drug.

After taking a deep dive into my past and asking the question, "Why do I get high on external validation?", I discovered that it was an unmet need from my childhood. My parents had struggled and that had made for a tumultuous upbringing. I grew up being in a constant state of trying to prove my worth, and I continued to do so throughout adulthood. COVID hit, and during the time that we were forced to stay inside, I followed through and went all the way in. I opened up Pandora's box to the past to understand why I was so hungry for validation, and what that said about me.

For years I had dreamed of writing a book. Finally I had all the time in the world, but I was overwhelmed with the feelings of not being good enough to perform the task. Negative thoughts festered inside of me on repeat, like a scratch on vinyl—the needle stuck in a groove and repeating the same sound over and over again like a mantra. You are not good enough! No one cares. Who is going to read your work anyway? Why bother? It all seems like a waste of time!

I refused to believe that those were the whispers of the universe. My logical brain knew that this was just noise because my heart had a book to write. A book that people would indeed read. Another project I could be proud of. My self-doubt was born of false narratives encoded into my being. I would need to figure out their roots in order to dismantle them. Time after time I kept asking, "Why, why, why do I think I am not good enough?" I questioned my beliefs. I reminded myself that I am an intelligent woman who has proven herself time and again. Yet, here I was stuck—and not doing something that I really wanted to do. I knew it was merely me getting in my own way. In order to move forward, I had to decode the why.

Unintentionally, I opened up old wounds from the past. The self-doubt had been bred from unresolved childhood traumas. I had to sit with my past to help me move forward. At the time, I didn't realize the enormity of what I was about to do. Once you see something, you can't unsee it. In the end, it would help me to see things that I had long buried but continued to carry like a fifty-pound backpack. In the process, I learned about ancestral trauma and the consequences of being raised by two emotionally unavailable parents. I had been a sensitive and intuitive child who had just wanted to be seen and heard. Oftentimes, I had been asked to deny myself in order to meet my parents' needs. I had been overcome with fear of abandonment. My father had carried this wound himself because his father had abandoned the family when my dad was only nine years old. My fear had been born in the dark hours of the night, when my dad took out his frustrations physically and verbally on my mom, coaxing her to leave. My little four-year old body had lain paralyzed, hoping that he would leave instead of her. I had needed my mom. Ironically, I still need my mom but she still doesn't see how.

Although the feelings of paralysis subsided, I never quite felt at home with my family. My dad remained verbally abusive and struggled to raise a teenage daughter; I can't tell you how many times he called me a bitch and made me feel stupid. He made me believe that that was true. I couldn't take it anymore so after high school, at seventeen years old, I saw an opportunity to leave. I moved in with my aunt to attend school in Lennoxville, a two-hour car ride from home. My intention was to break free and begin my own life. It was a fresh start.

In journeying into my past, I was able to extract the stories that I had adopted as my own—but that were never mine. My dad's unresolved traumas became part of my story. I am the product of my father's emotional volatility; I am an empathetic person who seeks to help fix others. I am also the product of my mother's insecurities; I am constantly riddled with self-doubt. Because of my upbringing, I would become my own worst critic, constantly self-sabotaging and self-abusing. As a little girl, I had been in constant fear of rocking the boat because the family unit had been so fragile. It had been far from a stable home.

I have forgiven myself and my parents for the past and it has helped me tremendously on my healing journey. It has helped me to accept the parts of me that I hadn't been able to before. It made me realize that so much of the shame that I had been carrying had never been mine—it belonged to my parents and my grandparents and maybe even to my great grandparents. Although going through this process was painful, it liberated me. I could now go forward and tell my story truthfully and authentically without yearning for outside validation of any kind.

Spiritual Awakening

Opening up to my past put me in touch with my spiritual side. It's a part of me that I knew existed but that I had chosen to ignore up until now. I had felt spirituality was something for nutty people. For the longest time I had perceived spiritual people as weird or fringe. When thinking about spirituality I had pictured witches in the forest dancing around a fire seducing the divine, a medium talking to people who have crossed over to the other side, or individuals visiting Peru to take ayahuasca.

Spirituality can be those things, but it can also be found in the everyday. A spiritual practice might include yoga, meditation, nutrition, astrology, reading, or mixing herbs. I was learning to shed my misconceptions. In fact, when I started to meditate, my mind started to expand and I opened myself up to the opportunities. A spiritual practice was the gateway to a whole new world of self-discovery. Getting in touch with my spiritual side would help me feel more myself—at times more complete. It was as though I had found the missing piece of the puzzle that would make me feel whole.

I would invest time in new practices: Reiki, grounding, forest bathing, crystals, and astrology. I would meet spiritual guides who would teach me to tap into deeper parts of myself. What I was learning was empowering. It was transformative and, at this point in my life, necessary. I was learning self-forgiveness with a level of love, respect, and compassion that I had never known. I was beginning to truly understand the power within. I was adopting a whole new way of seeing my life.

Tired of the "hustle," I continued to look for ways of being that were more natural to me. I then found a guide who helped me to reconnect with my monthly cycle. Her work involves helping women honour the divine feminine within by turning inward, rather than out of the body. I began to understand things about myself that I used to label as me just being depressed or lazy. I took the time to listen and heal myself before I tackled things outside of me. When I need food, I eat, when I am thirsty, I drink, and when I am tired, I sleep. Ignoring the body has consequences beyond the immediate.

Over the past few years, I have become a big podcast listener. During the height of the pandemic I discovered Lola Pickett and devoured her content. Her then podcast *Empath to Power* breaks down the meaning of being an empath and so much of it resonates with me. So much of what I thought were my "crazies" is shared amongst people who consider themselves empaths. I began to embrace the empath in me. I learned why I became tired so easily, felt other people's energies so much, and experienced generalized anxiety and sensory issues. For so much of my life I thought I was crazy, spending thousands of dollars on self-help books and therapy. Then I realised that I was pushing away parts of myself that I couldn't make fit with the people, places, and things that surrounded me. I didn't need to fit in—there was space for me to be me. Knowing this gave me a new sense of freedom. I was finally allowing myself to embrace all parts of me and not just those needing to fit in the way other people expected me to. In this process I learned to honour all parts of myself: the dark and the light, who I once was, and who I am. A true awakening.

I once thrived on spontaneity, but eventually I realized how depleting that had become to my nervous system. I thrived on intense hits of dopamine that would leave me feeling hungover afterward. When I said I was going to do something, I always followed through, even if it threatened to kill me. That is how I used to be, but not anymore. Now I prefer to proceed with caution and think before I jump into projects, make promises, or commit to things. So many parts of my past were born of snap decisions. In going forward I want to do things because they feel right for me. I want to feel grounded and at peace as much as possible. One of my favourite things is to rise with the sun with my cup of coffee in hand and thank the universe for a new day.

Barefoot

At one point during the summer of 2020 I was sitting on the dock of our rented cottage. I thought back to when I was a little girl. I grew up on a dirt road, and for the eleven years that I lived there, the road was never paved. At that time, it was uncommon to live on an unpaved road. The city workers passed every summer with grease trucks in an attempt to keep the dust clouds at bay. Looking back, I now understand my mom's obsession with washing windows. It must have driven her crazy—my clean-centric mom. We lived on an acre of land, so we had lots of room to run free, catch tadpoles, and swim. We had an extremely long driveway where I learned to ride my bike. They were simple times that were dotted with events that would shape who I am today. I love to go back in my mind to the long days of summer; BBQs with family friends; my grandparents visiting; and my favourite, driving the car of my maternal grandfather, Al, down the road while he sipped his beer in the passenger's seat. It was a different time.

Whatever I was doing, though, you could bet that I was walking around barefoot. (I can still feel the crab grass in between my toes and the jagged edges of the rocks threatening to pierce my skin.) I walked through puddles too, the oozing of brown goo between my toes squishy and warm. It felt weirdly comforting. I walked on surfaces when they were hot or cold. Walking across an asphalt-covered driveway on a hot August day, I swore it was going to peel the first layer of skin from the soles of my feet. A hop and an ouch—hop and an ouch—creeping along like the Grinch who stole Christmas. I still prefer not to wear shoes.

I may have owned a pair of slippers but I don't remember. Summer, winter, spring, or fall—my feet needed to be free. I still have yet to find a pair of socks that feels better than going bare. But something strange happens when we get older—suddenly our feet feel colder than they once did. Now in winter I am forced to layer up. I prefer socks over slippers, basically because I am clumsy as hell and trip over my own feet. Like a good face cream, I would pay any amount of money for a pair of socks that would warm my feet and make it feel like I wasn't wearing anything.

I was combing the internet to learn more about optimal health practices and I discovered something called grounding or earthing. I read an article that spoke of a man who never felt well when he travelled. He always felt out of sorts. I could relate because I felt the same. Whenever I travel, my preference is to stay in a boutique hotel because they are smaller. I always stay on one of the lower levels to avoid feelings of vertigo. Staying on a lower level helps me to avoid feeling off balance. Usually when I get off the elevator on a high floor I feel dizzy—as if I am going to fall down sideways. For the longest time I thought it was all in my head, but it was my body's strong desire to stay closer to the ground. The man in the article travelled frequently and brought a grounding mat with him everywhere he went. Within twenty-four hours of reading the article, I had a new grounding mat. The mat is reserved for when it's too cold outside to walk on the grass in my backyard. The simple act of connecting to the earth does indeed make me feel grounded. In discovering grounding, I have learned something about myself. Grounding is something that my body seeks naturally. Without naming it, I have naturally been doing something that my body yearns for. I have always known that I prefer my two feet planted firmly on the ground! This also says a lot about me when it comes to sport; I have dabbled in the world of triathlon. I like to swim, but mostly in a pool without worrying about pace or critters in the water. It took me years to feel okay with my feet clipped onto my bike, constantly worrying about losing control—especially on the downhills. The last leg, which is the run part in a triathlon, is when I feel my best. Nothing makes me happier than lacing up my running shoes! Again, one foot after the other striking the earth—this is where I feel most at home inside myself.

We had been at the cottage all week when my hubby called me to the dock. It seemed urgent so I quickened my steps; that's when I realized that I had spent the whole week walking barefoot. I giggled softly to myself because I knew that I had merely been doing what felt natural to me. Intuitively, I was doing for myself what my body needed. (It's important to slow down, put away the screens and listen to your body—it has a lot to tell you.) All week, my flip flops had been abandoned at the backdoor waiting for me to slip my feet in, but I had chosen to walk free.

I took advantage of our week at the cottage by waking early to see the sunrise, absorbing the soothing energy of the water, observing nature's creatures, taking a sound bath provided by the rain, and beholding the colours of the sky with the setting sun. I am beyond grateful for having spent a week nurturing myself in these small ways. Thank you mother earth for all of your gifts, and for helping me to realize that all of your offerings are an elixir for love, health, and healing.

Herculean Task

One of the hardest things we humans have to navigate is relationships. We have so many and all are navigated differently. It starts with our family and friends and then it extends to classmates, colleagues, and society at large. Early on we learn to take into consideration who we are, what we are looking for in others, and what we can provide for them in return. The best relationships are reciprocal until you get to parenthood. The relationship between parent and child is plainly one-sided until the child grows older and can make real contributions to the family. Until then, it's all about meeting their needs. Manisha has always been given chores to teach her responsibility. As time went on, her to-do list grew and her responsibilities varied. Unfortunately, the scale has never tipped for Keyan, and it never will. The relationship will always be one sided, with us doing for him.

I desperately wanted to be a mother and was saddened when that did not come easily. It took me over two years to become pregnant. We had countless interventions, therapies, and surgeries to get us to parenthood. We miscarried our first baby at about ten weeks. I had named him Aidan, although we did not know the sex; we hadn't gotten to the ultrasound yet. Soon after I became pregnant with Manisha. The day she was born was one of the happiest days of my life. Becoming a parent was something that I went into without expectation. My children were born out of love. They were not born to meet our unfilled desires. I didn't have children to succeed where I had failed. Kunal and I went into parenthood with the idea of taking the best of ourselves and passing it on by loving and nurturing our children, and also by encouraging them to be the best human beings that they could be.

Manisha has turned out to be the best of Kunal and I rolled into one. She is cerebral like her father and empathetic like her mama. She makes parenthood easy. Keyan, on the other hand, is like raising the ultimate narcissist. We give and we give and we give. Sometimes when I am shaving him I think, How is this my life?! This will always be my life until I die. There are times when I want to live to be one hundred years old so that I can care for Keyan, because I know no one else will love him the way we do. Then there are other days when I think of the unfairness of it all.

I look on social media at moms who are creating content on how and why it is overwhelming to be a mom. Then I think, Ladies, imagine having a child that will never grow up. That is my fucking reality. One day your kid will be in charge of their own personal hygiene, will learn to cook and care for themselves, and will move out. Every parent assumes that that is the natural flow. Not if you have a kid like Keyan. I have a hard time thinking beyond the immediate; if I do, I get depressed. If I am exhausted caring for Keyan now, what does that look like when I am much older? I know people think that at some point he will be placed in a home or a care facility; although that might possibly be true, we are still far away from that time. I couldn't imagine other people caring for Keyan full time while we are still alive. If I had to guess for how much longer I can care for Keyan on my own, I would say another ten years. That would bring Keyan to twenty-eight to thirty years old. His school years would be behind him which would mean that I would be taking care of him on my own for twenty-four hours a day, seven days a week. Right now he goes to school and is out of the house for seven hours a day. I can't even begin to imagine how I am supposed to cope with caring for him twenty-four hours a day on my own.

When I think about my life with Keyan and how I am his ultimate caregiver, I know I have been assigned a Herculean task. Keyan is Mount Everest brought into my life to challenge me in every way. I don't have a choice, he is mine to care for. I promised my children before they were born that I would give them the best of me. To this day I continue to uphold that promise. I have an extreme level of anxiety about Keyan's future; I find it difficult to put into words. It is like the moment you put on a harness for that bungee jump. As you're buckling into your harness your thoughts are all over the place. Your heart begins to beat faster and in order to stay calm you block out what is about to happen. Even if you take a more methodical approach to the jump by visualizing the steps, there remains a certain amount of fear. Despite preparing yourself the best that you can, the jump overwhelms you anyway; your heart leaps out of your throat as you yell on the way down. That is how I feel when I think about the future. Keyan's future is my future too.

Keyan's Service Dog

The MIRA foundation trains and donates service dogs to individuals with visual impairments, physical disabilities, and autism. We put Keyan's name on the list for a dog. Our hope was that the dog would help with Keyan's anxiety and ultimately help him sleep through the night. We waited two and a half years to get Bagou, a gorgeous black and white labernese. On September 13, 2015, after I had spent a week at the MIRA training camp, I brought Bagou home. We were thrilled to bring her into our family. Keyan still woke every night but he now had a buddy. Several times a week you could see our dog sandwiched between Kunal and Keyan as they walked down the street. And it is true that dogs undoubtedly become parts of our families. Many of us refer to them as fur babies. At times we may even like them more than our own children. We end up loving them fiercely and that is why I cannot publish my story without including this:

Dear Bagou,

I asked you repeatedly to tell me when it was time. The moment you stopped eating I knew. There were other subtle signs but not eating was the big one. That is when I placed the call to the vet's office. Since the beginning of the pandemic I have been fully exposed to all of my wounds. I have been on a path of spiritual awakening and you have been by my side, energetically supporting me. Knowing when I needed you to sneak up to bed with me. Initially you came into our lives to be of service to Keyan but in the end you really came to save me. The guardian of my emotions, you watched, guarded, and stood by me, your expressive eyes so attentive to my needs.

I protected you from Keyan's rejection. When he felt it necessary to run after you to make you scamper I always made sure you were safe. Okay, there were a few times you got a kick in the butt, but you knew the deal when you became a service dog. You were adopted from the MIRA foundation to help alleviate Keyan's sleep disturbances and overall anxiety. Things didn't work out according to plan, and unfortunately you didn't have the kind of impact we had hoped for. You were only in his room a short while before we realized that your presence was making things worse. After being with us for a few months, your health issues started. It was five years ago when they told us that you either had bowel issues or cancer. I never believed in cancer treatment for animals and so it was then that I decided to take your health into my own hands. They wanted to take a biopsy, but if they did, I risked losing you. You could have died while in surgery. I brought you home and started to make you homemade food. It helped alleviate your symptoms and it confirmed to me that you had a sensitive gastrointestinal tract. That is how we treated your first cancer scare. We would make sure that whatever time you had left would be the best! I granted you more grace to be a family dog convinced that extra love and affection would be good for your health. The second cancer scare in 2021 was real.

We were able to determine that it was cancer by a simple blood test this time. It was determined that you had bladder cancer and that you had a maximum of six months left with us. We celebrated your eighth birthday and then eleven days later we had to let you go. I thought you would be here much longer. This is when I fall apart. A gaping hole left in my heart by your departure.

I keep thinking of your eyes because that is where your soul communicated with mine. Your final day I felt your sheer exhaustion. As your mama, I wanted so desperately to take away your pain and transfer it over to me. I could feel your tiredness in your bones. When I asked the technician how long it takes for the sedative to set in, her response was, "Between five to fifteen minutes." Your exhaustion was so apparent it only took you two minutes to close your eyes for the last time. We took the time to be with you, to touch you, wanting you to feel our love and support in your transition. We cried and continued to pet you as you fell into a deep sleep. When I put my ear to your nose there was a gentle snore. I continued to remind you how much I loved you and what you meant to me.

Thirty-six hours have gone by since you passed away. I walk around the house missing your energy. That is how connected I felt to you. When I wasn't well, you would come check on me. I loved in the last months how you jumped on the white sofa and I would be startled to find you there. You were made to live in service to others but you had a rebel side to you. That was apparent once we received the diagnosis of cancer and we retired you from service. All the indulgences we allowed you! There was no holding you back—you went for it. I loved that we could cuddle on the sofa while watching TV. I watched people love you, particularly Uncle Bernie—I used to joke how he would make out with you. I could write a book on only you—a dog. My protector, my spirit animal, my baby dog.

Today is a beautiful sunny day and wanting to feel close to you I make my way outside. I listen to the birds and smile. When you were passing, I told you that I would hear you in the birds. Anytime I was in nature I would feel you, my beautiful beast. You were my four-legged fur baby, and all I wanted to do was care for you. It feels weird to not have to open the door thirty times a day. I don't miss cleaning up urine in the house. Last week you no longer had any control over your bladder. Kunal and I had even spoken about diapers. I wasn't going to do that to you, though. I was sensitive to your dignity. I would never have done that to you.

I asked you to tell me when it was time and you did. Every day for months I watched for subtle signs. When I called the vet six weeks prior to your death he said you were ready to go. I wasn't ready to let you go! I called the vet because I found blood in your urine. You and I both knew it wasn't yet time. You were stronger than that and I could see it in the wagging of your tail and the affection you continued to deliver. We only had six and a half years together and I wanted to ensure that you lived a beautiful life right up until the very last day. On March 31, 2022, Manisha, Kunal, and I sat with you until your last breath—we wanted to make sure that you felt the love we had for you.

Thank you Bagou.

Beads

Parents who have high-functioning, special needs children obsess about work integration. They want their adult children to have a place to go every day, to be around others, to make money, and to have a sense of purpose. I already know that Keyan would not be a good candidate for a work program. He doesn't have the desire to be helpful—there is no intrinsic motivation for him. He gets zero satisfaction from pleasing others (okay, maybe his mama once in a while). If he doesn't want to do something, he simply won't do it. He has no concept of money and therefore can't be motivated by it. He has a hard time sitting still, so concentration for him is difficult. Patience and focus are what they work on in school. I know my son well, and he needs a program that works around him rather than the other way around.

Having Keyan home during the first wave of COVID taught me a lot. With school shut down and his inability to follow online learning, I had no choice but to homeschool him. I placed a huge order of materials from Amazon and got working. I didn't want him to lose the gains he had made in school. The teachers sent us a video portfolio of Keyan's school work, so I was pretty confident that I could do this. I quickly realized that he loved it when we sat together to do puzzles. Every time we sat together I wondered, How does this apply to the real world? If only he could get a job putting puzzles together. Then I remembered the day in December after Kunal's company Christmas party. We had stayed in the city overnight, and the next day while roaming the shops of Old Montreal, I had stumbled upon a strand of raw wooden beads. I would later learn that they were called farmhouse beads. This was a time when I was obsessed with future plans for S.Au.S. I would envision the adults at our day center doing small jobs and projects as a way for them to continue to learn, grow, and potentially make money. I showed the beads to Kunal and told him that Keyan could do this. He agreed. Then I put the thought out of my mind until now when I was sitting at the kitchen table with Keyan.

One day while browsing Pinterest I came across farmhouse beads. There were several DIY projects with them. I could envision Keyan and I sitting together to do this. I had nothing to lose and decided to order the materials. Immediately, my creative brain imagined building a small business for Keyan. It could be an actual job for my son, or maybe he would handcraft Christmas gifts for the family.

The evening that I decided to bead with Keyan, I laid all the materials out on the kitchen table; I was overjoyed that it turned out to be an immediate success. He knew what to do because it was something that he had learned at a young age in occupational therapy to help with fine motor skills. As I watched Keyan's hands, I realized how important this practice would be to keep his fingers nimble. I prepared the string and handed him the beads; suddenly we were in business. He was interested and engaged. I was flabbergasted. We sat at the kitchen table for over twenty minutes. He radiated calm and I felt it too. We were working in unison—peacefully and happily.

Amazing! Here was something that my son and I could do together. I already knew that I wanted to call his small business Keyan's Way. Originally that is what I had wanted to call S.Au.S., but Kunal had said that it was too Anglo for Quebec, and of course he was right. This time I could use the name Keyan's Way because I would be selling his beads online, avoiding the crazy language laws.

Having lived for so many years in fear for his future, I felt as though I had figured it out. During the weeks that followed, my heart swelled with pride when I watched Keyan do his thing. He was often smiling while rocking back and forth and back and forth, all signs indicating that he was happy. Keyan doesn't get to do a lot with his hands. If I didn't place the scotch tape at the end of the string to properly move the bead through the hole, Keyan would ask for help. He did that by intertwining the fingers of one hand into the other. He was forced to practice patience while waiting for me to fix it. The activity was definitely strengthening his patience muscle. This was important to us since he is very impulsive and will jump up and run away without warning. I was constantly thinking of ways to break down this process to help maximize Keyan's independence. Eventually, I wanted him to do the work on his own. That was the ultimate end goal, and I knew it would take a while to get there.

I never imagined Keyan being able to contribute to his own livelihood. Should we open an Etsy shop for him, or create a website—maybe sell directly from Facebook? I never thought that this child would have the potential to make a dollar, and here I was trying to figure out the best marketing strategy. Life is full of surprises. I have seen parents create workplace environments for their special needs children such as car washes, cafés, and other small businesses, because no one else will hire them. The problem with Keyan is that his sensory issues paired with his anxiety makes it such that he can't function well in an environment where there is too much going on. It occurred to me that a simple and quiet life, like that of an artist, would be something more fitting to his temperament. Here I finally clued in that Keyan could do work if it was on his own in an environment that felt safe, calm, and quiet. As things progressed, I helped him less and less, wanting desperately to teach him that he could do this on his own. Independence was the goal. We made progress to the point where he beaded by himself while I scurried around the kitchen, cooking or washing dishes.

Soft Launch for Keyan's Way

We had the soft launch for Keyan's farmhouse beads. Albeit I was not 100 percent prepared, I advertised his new business on my Facebook page. I wanted to put out feelers for the product. The response was overwhelmingly positive. Over sixty beads were ordered on the first day. The next day, I had to hustle to get the order forms and payment options worked out. That was when I realized that I had to fine tune the business side of things. I didn't want to wait too long for the launch, because I wanted to get the beads into people's hands before the holidays. Making products by hand takes time and patience, especially when working with a craftsman who walks away whenever he feels like it. Getting everything organized by myself made me realize how labour intensive this was. After only two days, I was drained.

We decided as a family, or should I say, I insisted, that every family member would play a role in the business. Keyan would string the beads. I would assist by preparing the string, sorting the beads, and tying the knot. Kunal would work out all the ins and outs accounting-wise. He would also track on an Excel spreadsheet the name, address, and payments of Keyan's customers. I would take care of the marketing and whatever loose ends needed to be handled. Manisha would prepare the mailings. Keyan would make in-person deliveries to those who lived in the neighborhood, providing us with destinations for our daily drives.

After three months, Keyan's business did not go according to plan and we shut it down. Although he was successful in making and selling his beads, we learned that in order for Keyan to receive government benefits, he would not be allowed to collect money from any other source. If Keyan continued to sell beads, the government would be allowed to withhold his benefits. The rate at which he could make and sell beads would never sustain him. We had a choice to make. I want to highlight what is most important here. It's more than money. Keyan needs to be recognized in the government database as someone needing assistance. Collecting benefits now ensures that the government has Keyan in their system if and when there is an opportunity for him to attend a day program or to be placed in a residence in his old age.

Harmony

After turning the page on Keyan's Way, I allowed myself time to feel sad, frustrated, and discouraged. Once I got tired of wallowing in self-pity, I decided that the best approach moving forward was to shift my own mindset. Over the years, I have learned that so many things are out of my control. If I can't control the situation, then I *can* control the way I feel about it.

I again begin to obsess about Keyan's future. How can he and I live in harmony? I move from visualizing dropping him off at a day program to him being home with me, the days filled with small household tasks, running errands together, and learning through playing games. The word harmony has become my new mantra, and it anchors me so that I can think calm thoughts. I visualize us spending time in the pool or spa, exploring new painting techniques, and continuing to create content for social media for our autism awareness campaign. Thinking this way helps me to feel more in control and empowered. I have been able to carve out a beautiful life thus far, and I have to trust that I can manifest what comes next.

Having now given up the supermom façade, I knew I needed outside help. When I looked towards the future I already knew that I couldn't do it alone. Help would have to come in the form of caring for Keyan, and also in assistance with tackling the family to-do list: cooking, cleaning, and groceries. It's about finding the balance between taking care of Keyan and taking care of myself, too. Therefore, I am currently exploring things that we can do together that we both find joy in: walking; beading; painting; playing; and my favourite, taking naps together.

Living in Tandem

The end of another long journey. Holding this book in my hands, I feel all the emotions I did when I crossed the finish line in Boston back in April 2014. I am feeling all the feels, from pride to exhaustion. I know I will look back at this book and think that I should have included other stories, or maybe more of them, but the truth is, I can go on forever. It would mean never crossing the finish line.

My running journey has been a magical one, from running dirt roads in the country, to tree lined trails, to big city streets. I run in the most affluent neighbourhoods and the sketchiest parts of town. Those who know me well know that my preference is to be out under a blue sky, sun shining, with small cheering sections. Running has been my meditation, somewhat of a slow activity. I am able to see things clearly after a run—oftentimes it is where I find solutions to my problems.

There was a time when I ran with only one goal in mind and that was to finish the race; the more experience I gained, the more confident I became. I started lining up with the intention of winning the race or at least my age category. I became competitive, always wanting to be in the top 10 percent of female runners. I was thirsty for it! It was something that I could achieve in shorter races (five kilometers, ten kilometres, and half marathons) but not the marathon. I am proud to say that I was the first female to cross the finish line in a few local races. Getting a medal at the end of a race made me feel accomplished, but standing on a podium made me feel badass! I am especially proud since this girl was one who got chosen close to last in gym class and wasn't good enough to make any sports team in high school. I know I am uncoordinated, and that is why putting one foot in front of the other is what I do best.

Over the years, I have slowed down. During COVID I lost my mojo for running. Every time I laced up I felt heavy—and not just because of the few pounds that I had gained. It was something more. My legs felt like cement blocks that I couldn't propel forward. I started to accept that I could only put my energy into so many things at once. I was home with the whole family, focusing on my writing and healing past wounds. Natural aging and perimenopause also factored into the equation as to why I wasn't able to run. I now realized that everything changes—absolutely everything: our goals, our dreams, our jobs, our mindset, our perspective, our priorities, and our minds. Although the pandemic made it feel as though nothing was moving—everything was moving drastically for me.

I grew up on a dirt road, but that doesn't define me. I now live in one of the most affluent neighbourhoods in the suburbs of Montreal, but that doesn't define me, either. Runner, athlete, finisher, or winner may or may not define me; it depends on who you are asking. I went from the girl who never made the team, to the one leading the race or organizing it. I have now opted out of most of the races that I was in. I am no longer chasing my past, but healing from it. The Mount Everest that I thought I was climbing for Keyan—I am now walking around it. The places where I once desired to fit in, are far from the places where I now want to be. I have found my voice—not to scream with, but rather to whisper. Those who need to hear it will.

www.ingramcontent.com/pod-product-compliance
Lightning Source LLC
Chambersburg PA
CBHW061144120626
46546CB00005B/1926